Praise for
Facing the Fracture

"This book is a master class for every American exhausted by toxic division and looking for a way out. Dr. Israel offers a refreshingly evenhanded look at the challenge and empowers us with practical tools that quickly build resilience, strength, confidence, and hope."

—**PEARCE GODWIN**, founder, Listen First Project

"If you're feeling overwhelmed and even hopeless about our divided nation, don't give up. Read *Facing the Fracture*! Tania Israel's levelheaded, evidence-based ideas will leave you empowered and inspired, with a clear set of practical strategies for strengthening your family, community, and country."

—**JASON MARSH**, executive director, the Greater Good Science Center, UC Berkeley; editor in chief, *Greater Good*

"*Facing the Fracture* guides us toward a future where Americans can be more emotionally fortified, interpersonally skilled, and profoundly optimistic about our country. This important book provides a road map for personal empowerment, helping us overcome the stresses and challenges of our deeply polarized times."

—**JAMIE METZL**, founder and chair, OneShared.World; author, *Hacking Darwin: Genetic Engineering and the Future of Humanity* and *Superconvergence: How the Genetics, Biotech, and AI Revolutions Will Transform Our Lives, Work, and World*

"*Facing the Fracture* addresses the dilemma every sentient being wrestles with: how do we disagree with others without losing our minds? Wise, informed, openhearted, and revelatory, Tania Israel is onto something big. We're not as different as we think!"

—**ALAN WATT**, best-selling author, *Diamond Dogs* and *The 90-Day Novel: Unlock the Story Within*; founder, L.A. Writers' Lab

"Enlightening, empowering, and thoroughly entertaining! In helping us to control what we're confronted with, become resilient, and react meaningfully, Tania Israel offers clever insights, frequent grins, and the exact tools we desperately need right now. Above all, though, she gives us hope."

—**STARSHINE ROSHELL**, award-winning journalist; media literacy advocate

"At a moment of extreme division and polarization, Dr. Israel provides practical insights to find our common humanity with those we disagree with. As a Gen-Z member, I can confidently state that young people are looking to lead with empathy and hope—this book provides us with a great how-to guide."

—**MANU MEEL**, cofounder and CEO, BridgeUSA; host, *The Hopeful Majority* podcast

"In this candid and courageous book, Tania Israel offers a blueprint for finding greater fulfillment and connection in polarized times. I strongly recommend this book to fellow academics, students, and others navigating conflict and division. *Facing the Fracture* offers wisdom that we need right now."

—**TENELLE PORTER,** assistant professor,
Rowan University; intellectual humility researcher

"Tania Israel has provided us with a comprehensive and incredibly insightful understanding of polarization in our country. Readers of this treasure of a book will be informed, empowered, and optimistic about one's future and that of our nation. I strongly recommend this compelling and timely resource!"

—**MELBA J. T. VASQUEZ,** PhD, ABPP, former president,
American Psychological Association

"We are all too aware of how political polarization is fracturing our lives and how news avoidance threatens our civic duty. Dr. Tania Israel offers us hope and a road to engagement. She gives us original and practical ways of dealing with these issues in our day-to-day lives and provides a wealth of data that debunks what we think we know about our fellow citizens. To find out more, you'll have to read her eye-opening book . . . and I strongly recommend you do!"

—**DEANNA LEE,** former head of communications at the
Carnegie Corporation, The New York Public Library,
and the Asia Society; former senior producer, ABC News

"Although it feels like we are facing an impossible divide in this country, Tania Israel's new book offers an optimistic vision for navigating political hostility. She debunks myths about polarization, corrects our distorted perceptions, and lays out a scientific framework for opening minds and bridging divides."

—**JAY VAN BAVEL,** professor of psychology and neural science, New York University; coauthor, *The Power of Us: Harnessing Our Shared Identities to Improve Performance, Increase Cooperation, and Promote Social Harmony*

"Worried about politics? You could duck and hide and hope it will blow over, or you can read this book."

—**LISA SWALLOW,** cofounder and executive director, Crossing Party Lines, Inc.; author, *Yes, You CAN Talk Politics*

"Many of us feel discouraged, if not hopeless, about bridging the gap with people who have opposing political opinions. Dr. Tania Israel has provided us with a gift in the form of a highly readable book that is full of actionable tips that, when followed, increase the likelihood of beneficial conversations across political lines. I am so grateful to her—you will be too."

—**ADAM DORSAY,** PsyD, licensed psychologist; host of the award-winning *SuperPsyched* podcast

"Not only does America need Dr. Tania Israel's strategies for reducing polarization, but—maybe more importantly—we need her clear-eyed optimism. Word by word, sentence by sentence, *Facing the Fracture* helps us deconstruct what divides us, teaches us how to listen and, ultimately, how to heal."

—**BETH MACY**, *New York Times* best-selling author, *Dopesick: Dealers, Doctors, and the Drug Company that Addicted America*

"Tania Israel's new book is a primer for the politically perplexed. In clear, clever, cogent writing Israel argues for empathy and care while seeking engagement with others we see as different. The book offers many practical suggestions to prepare ourselves to engage, as well as actually talk the talk and walk the walk through dialogue and bridgebuilding for the future. A useful guide for all citizens!"

—**SHERYL BOWEN**, PhD, faculty director, Dr. Terry Nance Center for Dialogue, Villanova University

FACING the FRACTURE

How to Navigate the Challenges of Living in a Divided Nation

Tania Israel, PhD

GREENLEAF
BOOK GROUP PRESS

Published by Greenleaf Book Group Press
Austin, Texas
www.gbgpress.com

Distributed by Greenleaf Book Group

For ordering information or special discounts for bulk purchases, please
contact Greenleaf Book Group at PO Box 91869, Austin, TX 78709,
512.891.6100.

Design and composition by Greenleaf Book Group and Mimi Bark
Cover design by Greenleaf Book Group and Mimi Bark
Cover image used under license from ©Shutterstock.com/Jozef Micic

Publisher's Cataloging-in-Publication data is available.

Print ISBN: 979-8-88645-234-1

eBook ISBN: 979-8-88645-235-8

To offset the number of trees consumed in the printing of our books,
Greenleaf donates a portion of the proceeds from each printing to the
Arbor Day Foundation. Greenleaf Book Group has replaced over 50,000
trees since 2007.

Printed in the United States of America on acid-free paper

24 25 26 27 28 29 30 31   10 9 8 7 6 5 4 3 2 1

First Edition

WE THE PEOPLE—
I HAVE FAITH IN US

Contents

Introduction

The symptoms crept up in the months leading up to the 2016 election. It started with trouble falling asleep. This was unusual. I have always been a very good sleeper. But in summer 2016, my brain was busy, chattering with political commentary about Hillary Clinton vs. Donald Trump. In my head were NPR reporters, local activists, social media posts, friends and family who turned to me with their fears.

Lying in bed with a busy mind and no mental snooze button, I tried listening to my favorite playlists of relaxing music. Lyrical tunes distracted me from the political chatter in my brain, but only momentarily. Soon, the music became a background soundtrack for a steady stream of prognosticating the outcome and consequences of the upcoming election. I needed a stronger antidote, and I found my salvation in the musical *Hamilton*. Not known for its relaxing qualities, the *Hamilton* cast recording nonetheless gave me what I needed—words, words, and more words to drown out the voices in my brain that would not shut up. By November, I knew the show by heart.

Like many Americans, I was suffering from living in a fractured nation. For many of us 2016 was an awakening to the extent to which the United States was divided. The situation has continued to deteriorate in the years that followed. In fact, two-thirds of Americans cite the current political climate as a significant source of stress.[1] Although my solidly Blue bubble of friends and family largely buffers me from interpersonal conflict, 19 percent of Americans have had a recent political disagreement that hurt their relationship with family or friends,[2] and 15 percent have lost a friendship due to politics.[3]

I'm not telling you anything you don't know by saying that political conflict is rampant in our country. Many experience it as an existential threat to self, community, and democracy. What's less clear is how to face the challenges of living in a polarized society. After the 2016 election, I took to heart the factious consequences that Americans were experiencing. As a researcher, as a psychologist, and as an optimist, I set out to understand how to support people struggling with these persistent divides. My path began long before 2016, but in the focused work that followed, it developed into a journey that led me to write a book to help you navigate these fraught times.

FROM POLITICAL CONFUSION
TO POLITICAL COMMITMENT

When I was in seventh grade, I wasn't allowed to eat Nestlé Crunch bars. Actually, I wasn't allowed to eat any Nestlé products, but the only thing I really cared about was Nestlé Crunch bars, which are undeniably delicious. My parents were boycotting Nestlé,[4] who was marketing baby formula to women in Africa—even though these mothers had perfectly good (and free and antibody-fortified) milk in their breasts, and then the women couldn't afford to keep buying the formula, and they had stopped producing breast milk, and so the women were watering down the formula, and babies were dying of malnutrition . . . or something like that. What I understood at twelve years old was that Nestlé was causing babies to die in Africa—obviously a very bad thing. One day in the school lunchroom, a friend was eating a Nestlé Crunch bar, and I tried to explain to the table of my peers why this was a problem. At that point, my limited understanding of the impact of a multinational corporation in developing countries became evident. My convoluted attempts to articulate the rationale for the boycott confounded my friends, and I got more and more worked up, frustrated with my inability to convey the urgency of the situation.

As the child of academics who read the *Washington Post* daily and discussed current affairs over dinner, I, perhaps, should have been better informed about politics. I was, however, more interested in Nancy Drew and *Star Wars* than in Nancy Reagan and the Cold War. As a teen, I knew every word of every song on Pat Benatar's *Crimes of Passion*, but I knew little about "get tough on crime" policies. Politics was not my passion.

I went on to major in and then teach women's studies, which provided me with a lens for analyzing politics as it pertained to systems of inequity, but I remained underinformed about political parties and systems of government. Although I voted in every election from the age of eighteen and went to some protests, I wasn't actively engaged in politics for most of my adult life. I listened to NPR each morning, so I had a sense of the national news scene, but I would phone a friend on Election Day for guidance on local elections and ballot measures.

Everything changed for me when I heard Barack Obama speak in 2007. Sitting on a grassy hill at my local community college, I was enraptured by his stump speech. I didn't know where Darfur was, but his comments about it made me cry. It was a powerful reaction, but, on its own, not enough for me to commit to his campaign. Then I listened to his treatise, *The Audacity of Hope*, and, inspired by Obama's ability to bridge divides, I knew I wanted to live in a country led by this man. I attended a volunteer meeting, learned to canvass the next week, and then I rocketed from interested voter to engaged activist. I started the first neighborhood team for Obama in my town, and within three months, I was team coordinator for the local primary campaign. I went on to become a delegate to the Democratic National Convention, a member of my county's Democratic Central Committee, and a volunteer for local campaigns.

Despite my increased comfort in the political world, it was often stressful. Politics pitted two or more sides against each other, with only one possible winner, so conflict was inevitable. Every decision seemed consequential enough to impact an entire community or country, or to alienate a political friend or ally. Nonetheless, I felt empowered having skills to make a difference, and I did my best to bridge the Bernie-Hillary rift within Democratic circles. By the time of the 2016 election, I was highly engaged, a little bit stressed out, and unfailingly optimistic.

THE 2016 ELECTION

I have to admit, I was floored by the results of the 2016 presidential election. In my progressive bubble of activist friends, and liberal intellectual family and colleagues, not only did I not know anyone who was voting for Donald Trump, but I also didn't know anyone who wasn't openly horrified at the idea of a Trump presidency. The podcasters I listened to poked fun at him, and when the tape about grabbing women's genitals surfaced, it was received gleefully by those who assumed this would tank any chance of him winning.

Confident in the presidential contest, I then turned to the local elections I cared about: friends running for city council and state ballot measures that mattered. And so, after work on Election Day, I was wearing a pantsuit and knocking on doors, getting out the vote in the student community next to my campus. Every so often I came across someone who wanted guidance on the ballot measures or needed to know their voting location. Canvassing was like playing a slot machine; the intermittent reinforcement kept me going. I wasn't paying attention to early returns from the East Coast until I came across an apartment full of college students watching TV and cheering as states were called in Trump's favor. I dismissed this scene as an anomaly and went to the local Democratic Party election night gathering. As the evening progressed, spirits were falling, but I, undaunted, continued plunking Hillary stickers on everyone and saying, "it's not over yet." I went to bed that night with *Hamilton* in my ears, clinging to my illusion that Hillary might pull through.

I managed my initial postelection overwhelm by taking long road trips, on which I listened to the biography about Alexander Hamilton that inspired the musical. This story, set in the late 1700s to early 1800s, offered me some insight into the political divisions that surfaced in the early years of the United States. Urban and rural interests, Southern and Northern economies, the rights of Black people, women's role in society, corruption, reputation, unreliable news—it was all there from the founding of our country. Conflict had always been present in our democracy, but was there a way we could resolve it without duels? Might there be a place for dialogue?

I was familiar with the healing potential of dialogue. More than twenty years earlier, I had started a group to bring together pro-choice and pro-life people to talk with each other. It was a transformational experience for me, not because it changed how I felt about abortion, but because it changed how I felt about people who disagreed with me about abortion. It offered me insight into values, thoughts, and experiences that humanized the opposition and helped me honor and respect their perspectives. I carried this learning into my work on LGBTQ issues, including conversations about religion and training for law enforcement. I was open to alternative viewpoints, and I felt it made me a more effective advocate. Nonetheless, I had clearly missed something—how could I and everyone I knew be so shocked that so many Americans supported Donald Trump? Clearly, there was a divide in our nation—not only in terms of voting and values, but also in terms of communication and understanding. Was there something I could do to help myself and others connect across the divide?

BEYOND YOUR BUBBLE AND BEYOND

In the wake of the 2016 election, I started generating resources to help people connect across the political divide. As a psychologist who was engaged in politics and had been teaching healing skills for twenty years, I thought I might have something helpful to offer. After developing *The Flowchart That Will Resolve All Political Conflict in Our Country*, I started offering a dialogue skills workshop, which led me to write a book, *Beyond Your Bubble: How to Bridge the Political Divide, Skills and Strategies for Conversations That Work.*

When *Beyond Your Bubble* was released in August 2020, in the midst of the Trump-Biden showdown, I thought my work on bridging political divides would be irrelevant after Election Day.

The Flowchart That Will Resolve All Political Conflict in Our Country

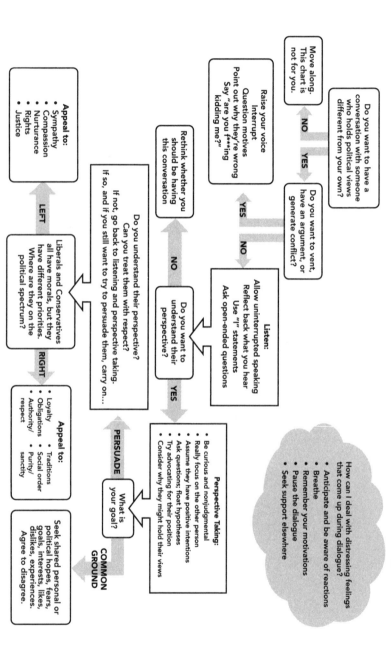

Do you want to have a conversation with someone who holds political views different from your own?

NO → Move along. This chart is not for you.

YES → **Do you want to vent, have an argument, or generate conflict?**

YES → Raise your voice / Interrupt / Question motives / Point out why they're wrong / Say "are you f***ing kidding me?"

NO → **Listen:** Allow uninterrupted speaking / Reflect back what you hear / Use "I" statements / Ask open-ended questions

Do you want to understand their perspective?

NO → Rethink whether you should be having this conversation

YES → **Perspective Taking:**
- Be curious and nonjudgmental
- Really focus on the other person
- Assume they have positive intentions
- Ask questions; float hypotheses
- Try advocating for their position
- Consider why they might hold their views

Do you understand their perspective? Can you treat them with respect? If not, go back to listening and perspective taking. If so, and if you still want to try to persuade them, carry on...

What is your goal?

PERSUADE / COMMON GROUND

Liberals and Conservatives all have morals, but they have different priorities. Where are they on the political spectrum?

LEFT → **Appeal to:**
- Sympathy
- Compassion
- Nurturance
- Rights
- Justice

RIGHT → **Appeal to:**
- Loyalty
- Obligations
- Social order
- Authority/ respect
- Traditions
- Purity/ sanctity

COMMON GROUND → Seek shared personal or political hopes, fears, goals, interests, likes, dislikes, experiences. Agree to disagree.

How can I deal with distressing feelings that come up during dialogue?
- Anticipate and be aware of reactions
- Breathe
- Remember your motivations
- Pause the dialogue
- Seek support elsewhere

http://taniaisrael.com/dialogue-flowchart/

But then came January 6 and vaccine hesitancy and gender ideology and Supreme Court decisions about abortion, affirmative action, and religious freedom . . . It seemed like every week, there was another topic that further divided the United States. It has become clear that my work will remain relevant as political polarization continues to stir up our emotions and deepen the cracks in our society.

Writing a book about how to have dialogue across political lines provided me with amazing opportunities. I was invited to be a guest on dozens of podcasts. I was interviewed by some of the most respected journalists in the business. I was quoted in the *New York Times*, the *Washington Post*, NPR, CNN, and other national and local news outlets. I made an appearance with Hoda and Jenna on the *Today* show. I trained state legislators and spoke on college campuses, at corporations, in churches, and at professional conferences. Furthermore, I was brought into the fold of other individuals and organizations that were working to bridge the political divide. And I got to hear from people who read *Beyond Your Bubble*. The conversations I had with readers confirmed what I had written in the book, and helped me to hone and advance my thinking. It was clear that dialogue could be valuable; however, it was also clear that dialogue wasn't sufficient to carry people through the trials of political polarization.

One of the greatest challenges to dialogue is the lack of desire to engage with political adversaries. A friend told me she bought *Beyond Your Bubble*, but she hadn't read it because then she might have to talk to "those people." Like this friend, I heard people consistently vilify those across the political spectrum, drawing on stereotypes that are highlighted in the media but unsupported by science. I've heard many people describe their attempts to connect across the political divide, and their frustration, pessimism, and distress are palpable.

The tools for dialogue that I offered in *Beyond Your Bubble* remain useful and evidence-based—and other excellent books have been published on bridging the divide—but it became clear to me that people need tools to enhance their peace of mind, whether or not they choose to engage across political differences. Looking for a broader set of resources, I found material about political conflict embedded in books about a wide variety of topics, written by a range of authors from journalists to organizational psychologists to Buddhist nuns. However, I could not locate a volume that brought together guidance from a breadth of sources to help people navigate the myriad challenges that arise in our minds, our hearts, and our interactions in a politically polarized world. So, I set out on a journey—compiling data, wisdom, and stories to meet the current need. My efforts resulted in this book—a guide to help Americans face these difficult and divisive times with confidence and courage.

THE PATH FORWARD

If you are feeling demoralized by the lack of a clear path forward, you're not alone. Americans are struggling to maintain their relationships, optimism, and equilibrium. As people voice woes about political conflict, several themes emerge that serve as my guideposts for this book.

First, given the complex institutional contributors to polarization, Americans are feeling disempowered. In the face of gridlock in Washington, biased news, and toxicity of social media, we may feel powerless as individuals to tackle the seemingly insurmountable challenges of political polarization. To be sure, we can point to public figures and corporations that are contributing to the problem. However, most of us are not elected officials, media conglomerates, or owners of social media platforms, so we have limited ability to make change on this larger level. We can, however, make decisions about how we interact with or consume messages from these sources, and we can shift how our minds process polarizing input to mediate its impact. That's what we'll focus on in Part I of this book.

It's also clear that Americans are exhausted from withstanding the bombardment of negative, conflictual, and threatening environmental influences. Shoring up our psychological capacity is key to an effective survival strategy. In particular, we benefit from resilience tools that help us tolerate difficult emotions. Our internal reactions to people who are different from ourselves are highly activated by the images and experiences of political conflict. We feel safer and stronger if we prepare our bodies, minds, and hearts for growth, as we will in Part II.

A final theme addressed in Part III is that political polarization increases isolation and contributes to it. Even if dialogue across political lines isn't the answer to everything, it will help us to repair ruptured relationships and build connections for support, collaboration, and advocacy. Beyond one-on-one associations, community connectedness supports feelings of belonging and can promote meaningful engagement. Even for those who do not want to participate, learning about the burgeoning bridge-building movement can serve as a beacon of optimism, and can offer opportunities to repair our country for people who are motivated to do so.

Political polarization presents us with challenges that threaten our health, our relationships, and the fabric of our country. But challenge is not necessarily only an obstacle; it can also serve as an opportunity for growth. These divided times may offer us a chance to develop a clearer view of ourselves, our communities, and our country. We might hone our psychological and interpersonal skills. This might be the moment that pushes us to achieve our individual and collective potential. My aim is for you to finish this book feeling informed, empowered, and optimistic about your future and the future of our nation.

HOW THIS BOOK CAN HELP

Each chapter will focus on a particular challenge that arises from and contributes to political polarization, and what you can do about it. It will reveal the root of the problem, as well as strategies to help you navigate specific aspects of our fractured society. Ultimately, the content of this book will equip you with knowledge, skills, and relationships that will empower you to take action, individually or with others, to strengthen yourself and your family, community, and country.

Part I: Reducing Polarizing Input

Chapter 1, "Get the Facts about Polarization," will provide accurate information about the political landscape. It will distinguish between ideological polarization and affective polarization— providing a clear picture of our differences, similarities, and misperceptions.

Chapter 2, "Consume News Wisely," will orient you to the impact of the twenty-four-hour news cycle on the media consumer. You will learn to recognize the limited perspective your preferred news source is offering, and you will strategize how to stay informed while limiting exposure to toxic, biased, and fake news.

Chapter 3, "Use Social Media Intentionally," will illustrate how social media platforms and the people who use them exacerbate societal divisions. You will learn some simple tips for using social media in ways that align with your goals and your health.

In Chapter 4, "Correct Distorted Perceptions," you will learn about cognitive biases that lead us to see people across the divide as extreme, uninformed, irrational, and immoral. Knowing how your mind works will put you in a position to counteract these human tendencies to distort reality.

Part II: Building Individual Capacity

In Chapter 5, "Foster Emotional Resilience," you will learn about the physiological response to political conflict, as well as the ways in which avoidance and outrage weaken us. You will find guidance to help you tolerate and grow from facing challenging political situations.

Chapter 6, "Broaden Your Mind," will help you harness curiosity and respect to open yourself to views that are different from your own. You will learn the benefits of perspective taking, and practice viewing things through multiple lenses. This chapter will stretch your mind and broaden your view.

In Chapter 7, "Open Your Heart," you will find strategies for cultivating empathy and compassion in the midst of disagreement. Employing guided meditation and other tools may put you in a state of mind that's eager to connect across the political divide.

Introduction

Part III: Strengthening Connection

Chapter 8, "Engage Effectively across the Divide," will help you harness the powers of curiosity, listening, and storytelling in your interactions with people who have contrasting ideologies and values. You will learn to navigate the challenges of moral frameworks, conflicting facts, and power differences to maintain relationships and deepen understanding.

Chapter 9, "Participate Meaningfully in Community and Country," will help you connect to other Americans on a local level and beyond. You will learn about threats to democracy and ways you can strengthen our systems of government. It will make evident why you cannot spell "United States" without *U* (you) and *I* and *US*.

Chapter 10, "Join the Bridging Movement," will reveal individuals and organizations who are working to knit our country back together. This chapter will show you what the media is not highlighting—successful efforts to bridge the political divide!

The conclusion, "Ready to Be Strong," will encourage you to achieve your potential. Knowledgeable, resilient, and connected, you have all you need to thrive in the face of political polarization.

Before you read on, I should confess something. Despite my increased knowledge about and engagement with politics, I'm still my adolescent self at heart. I remain drawn to movies and songs and TV and musical theater. Honestly, most of the podcasts in my playlist are about TV shows from the 1990s. Everyone assumes I follow *Pod Save America*, but I'm more likely to have *Buffering the Vampire Slayer* in my ears. As will become evident throughout this book, cultural touchstones and stories offer me comfort and inspiration. I hope you'll find that they do the same for you as I weave stories into this book to illustrate some of the major themes that guide our journey together.

PART I

Reducing Polarizing Input

From the most ancient legends to last week's reality TV, conflict is central to stories. There's a story that the news and social media and our minds have been feeding us about the state of our country. The story is one of good versus evil—you are good; they are evil. This is a compelling narrative. We certainly want to think of ourselves on the side of righteousness and justice against an oppressive and corrupt enemy.

The chapters that follow make a big ask—don't get caught up in the narrative of conflict; adjust your perspective to have a more accurate understanding of the political landscape. In Part I of this book, you will gain accurate knowledge of polarization, learn how to modify your news and social media consumption to turn down the volume on toxic input, and recognize your brain's role in distorting images of yourself and people across the political spectrum.

Rewriting this conflict narrative entails not only a change of view, but also a change of behavior. You might have fallen into patterns that aligned with the conflict story—keeping the news on in the background while you work or eat dinner, unthinkingly sharing memes that demean political adversaries, reveling in your superior intelligence and morality. Breaking habitual patterns helps us regain control over actions that have become automatic.[1] It's not always easy to shift out of well-worn patterns, but the payoff is mighty.

Perhaps an analogy will demonstrate this point. "Food deserts" are geographic areas with limited healthy nutritional options, where fruits and vegetables are lacking, but processed and fast foods high in sugar, fat, and salt are abundant. It's not that food isn't available; it's that the most accessible food will harm your body more than nourish it. Similarly, it's easy to locate and consume entertainment and news content that distorts reality, activates your destructive emotions, and fragments your relationships, community, and country. The more we feed on this content, the less space is available in our hearts and minds for accurate, grounding, and healing matter.

Similarly, we can consider consuming politically polarizing input in terms of smoking cigarettes. In both cases, you are taking in toxic materials. Your behavior is reinforced by the pleasure they provide, so you participate on a regular basis until you are at its mercy. Spending time with others who similarly enjoy the habit further reinforces the unhealthy behavior and makes it hard to quit.

Quitting smoking is not easy, nor is limiting your intake of politically polarizing input. But both changes are freeing. Modifying your intake will free you from the grip of political and corporate forces. It will free you from the damage to your body, mind, and spirit. It will free you to make your own choices about how to spend your attention, time, and money. It will free you to control your own destiny.

I'm a few decades behind in movie viewing, so I saw *Rocky* only recently. In case you missed this timeless film, the main character, Rocky Balboa, is a boxer. At the start of the movie, he smokes and drinks his way home to his small apartment, where his roommates are turtles and his fridge is a food desert of soda and donuts. As he shifts into training mode, he wakes up at 4:00 a.m., downs a high-protein drink (OK, it's just a bunch of raw eggs), and goes for a solitary run, ending his route limping up the steps of the Philadelphia Museum of Art. In an iconic training montage, Rocky works hard, punching a bag and animal carcasses, doing one-armed push-ups, withstanding hits to his body, and finally leaping up the art museum steps with energy to spare.

Rocky showcases the benefits of hard work, determination, and persistence. If we're going to shift out of an ongoing narrative of conflict, we'll also want to learn how to overcome hurdles we'll face daily. Motivation is necessary to set us in the direction of healthy behaviors, but it is generally not sufficient to get us past the physiological and psychological resistance to change.[2] You have to believe your efforts will make a difference, not necessarily in changing the world, but at least in changing your personal experience of external events. I have a lot of optimism about our ability to shift our behaviors, but belief isn't enough; one of the most helpful paths to change is developing a habit. Habits are enduring and can be supported with cues, other people, and rewards.[3] For example, to complete this book, I programmed my reminders app to prompt me to write each day, set up writing dates with a friend on WhatsApp video, and signed up for a daily writing challenge with prizes.

So, here I am, taking a metaphorical cigarette out of your mouth, reminding you, "You're in training," instilling in you the knowledge that, if you are stuck in a rut of consuming polarizing input, you are holding yourself back from achieving your potential. Putting your energy into activities that are not worthy of your attention and investing in toxic content that tears at your emotional and relational well-being is a trap.

The first phase of your training is weaning yourself off familiar patterns that have been comforting but are simultaneously harmful. Polarizing thoughts and media are junk food. A steady diet of nothing but mac and cheese is very satisfying in small doses, but is best accompanied by a vegetable or two lest it clog your arteries and restrict flow of lifeblood to your heart. Part I of this book is about reducing polarizing input from media, social media, and your own mind. This is about developing healthy habits of consumption that will offer you a healthier mental and media diet.

CHAPTER 1

Get the Facts about Polarization

Spoiler alert I'll be making a case in the chapters that follow that we are not as polarized as we think we are. In fact, news, social media, and cognitive biases are distorting our perceptions of people on the other side of the divide, and of political polarization itself. Since I'm going to tell you what we're getting wrong, I'd like to start by offering a baseline of factual information about polarization that you can compare with what you're hearing from the news, social media, and your own mind.

First, it's helpful to know that there are two types of polarization. Ideological polarization refers to the distance between our opinions, whereas affective polarization is how we feel about people who hold those other opinions.

IDEOLOGICAL POLARIZATION

Ideological differences have existed since the United States was established. For example, intense debates over slavery, federal versus state control, financial systems, and foreign relations were evident among the founders of our country. Discord in the late 1800s manifested in ugly political battles and a civil war. Although the current division is not the first or the bloodiest, it signals a clear and increasing schism that threatens the function and fabric of our society.[1]

Over the past several decades, Republicans and Democrats (and those who lean toward one party or the other) increasingly disagree about a wide range of issues, including immigration, government assistance, racial discrimination, and environmental regulation. In fact, differences of opinion based on political party are considerably larger than those due to age, religion, race, education, or gender.[2] So, yes, there are differences of opinion between those on the Left and Right, and as groups, the opinions are getting further apart.

Furthermore, partisans' opinions are increasingly consistent with either a conservative or liberal agenda. Rather than forming nuanced, issues-based views, opinions conform to the party line.[3] Nevertheless, these differences are not absolute. We may imagine people in the two major parties as polar opposites, but in fact, their views invariably overlap. For example, although QAnon is associated with the political Right, 10 percent of Democrats agree with QAnon ideology, and more than 70 percent of Republicans do not.[4] There is also no issue on which 100 percent of Democrats agree while no Republicans do.

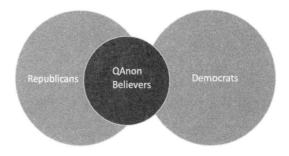

AFFECTIVE POLARIZATION

Although the increasing gap in Americans' views may feel disconcerting, within a healthy democracy, differences of opinion are to be expected, even encouraged. What seems more corrosive to our society than ideological polarization is affective polarization, the animosity we feel toward people on the other side of the political spectrum.

In-Group/Out-Group Dynamics

It's basic human nature to have warm feelings toward people in your own group, those with whom you share a trait or interest, and to feel antipathy toward those outside your group. Group identity can be based on a wide range of characteristics, including race, religion, profession, or school. I experienced this phenomenon when I started going to baseball games.

I must admit, I've never been much of a sports fan. I don't always follow what's happening, and I tend to cheer whenever either team does something exciting, which frustrates die-hard fans around me. Nonetheless, when a friend invited me to a Dodgers game, I took her up on the offer. It seemed like a pleasant way to spend a summer evening outdoors with good company. Not only did it live up to these expectations, but I also discovered that at the stadium concessions I could purchase nachos in a hat!

My friend kept extending invitations, and I kept accepting. After a few games, I started to pay more attention to what was happening in the game—I cheered for the right team, I knew the chants and songs, and I started wearing Dodger blue. I found that my interest in the team gave me something to bond with friends and coworkers over. I would poke my head into my coworker Maria's office and debrief last night's game. I watched at home with one of my besties, who was a longtime fan and helped me understand the finer points of the game and the personalities of the players. By the time the Dodgers lost the World Series, I was heartbroken for my team and outraged at the Houston Astros. I was experiencing the classic phenomenon of in-group favoritism and out-group derogation.

Tribal Politics

In-group/out-group dynamics of political division are sometimes described as "tribal." This terminology references the origins of human society; for most of history, we lived in small, cooperative groups. A key strategy for survival was to gain the favor of those in your tribe and eschew strangers, who potentially threatened your own and your group's existence. These instincts have become hard-wired into our psychology and are playing a key role in political polarization.

In-Group / Out-Group Bias

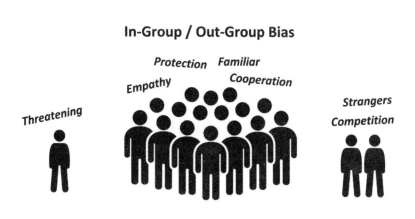

Living within these small groups, people's life-or-death distinctions between allies and enemies relied on the ability to identify those within and outside your tribe. It turns out that many tools of early human development remain with us today. This deep-rooted tribal drive underlies contemporary displays of political markers. Partisan identity is evident as people announce their affiliation on hats, bumper stickers, and dating profiles.[5] As politics have become more connected to identities, the people in your camp have become your tribe. As such, defending one's side and attacking the other feels like a battle for survival.

As Amy Chua describes in *Political Tribes*, "The Left believes that right-wing tribalism—bigotry, racism—is tearing the country apart. The Right believes that left-wing tribalism—identity politics, political correctness—is tearing the country apart. They are both right."

Given the powerful effect of group identity, it's no surprise that affiliation with a political party gives rise to affective polarization. In order to determine how people feel toward others within and outside of their political party, researchers have developed a number of methods: a "feeling thermometer" (how warm or cold you feel toward someone on a 0–100 scale), social distance (comfort interacting with others), traits associated with partisans (e.g., hypocritical, intelligent, open-minded), or behaviors (e.g., evaluation of job candidates). In all these studies, positive associations with one's own party and negative associations with the other party are evident.[6] It appears that the main driver of increased polarization is greater negativity toward people in the other party; positive feelings toward political compatriots have remained stable over time.[7]

Republicans and Democrats question the other party's intelligence, morality, and open-mindedness, and they believe the policies of their opponents are harmful to the country.[8] Few cross-party friendships can withstand such hostile environments, and fissures tear at our social fabric. Increasingly disgruntled by the idea of working with, living near, or having family members marry someone in a different political party, we sort ourselves into social bubbles of like-minded people.[9]

MISCONCEPTIONS

A key driver of affective polarization is misconceptions about what the other party believes and values, who they are, and how much they care about politics. And yet, despite these misconceptions and the growing ideological and social divide, Americans are far more united than we think we are. We may form errors in our thinking based on public statements made by politicians. It turns out elected officials don't provide an accurate picture of the general public—everyday citizens are not as divided as the people who represent them in government.[10]

They're Not as Extreme as You Think They Are

One common misconception about the political landscape is the extent to which we believe people are at the extremes. Decades of research consistently shows that Republicans and Democrats perceive each other as holding more extreme views than they actually do. This bias is evident in numerous studies, including thirty years of data from the American National Election Study.[11] With over 20,000 responses, and on every issue from national defense to women's rights, Democrats' and Republicans' views are not as far apart as people estimate them to be. Although there are people on the far ends of the spectrum, in general, people are probably not as extreme as you might imagine them to be.

It might be easier to demonstrate this with some visuals. This is how we might typically think about ideological polarization, which is also how it tends to be presented in the media. There are people on the Left, and there are people on the Right, and that's all there is.

Political Polarization: How We Think It Is

Left   **Right**

However, studies show that two-thirds of Americans are actually in between the extremes. More in Common, an organization that studies political views, calls them "The Exhausted Majority."[12] These people are less ideological, recognize complexity of issues, and support compromise. Notably, they are less likely to vote, and when they do, they are not consistently aligned with either side. They're also tired of political conflict and feel overlooked. They don't participate because they don't feel confident in their voice, they question if they can have an impact, or they have other priorities in their lives. When we focus only on people who voice positions strongly at either end of the political spectrum, we neglect the experiences and wants of this large constituency.

Political Polarization:
What the Data Show

Left   **Exhausted Majority**   **Right**

But wait, there's more. If you bend the political polarization continuum, you get a picture of an additional dimension of the political spectrum.

Political Polarization:
A New View

Left   **Exhausted Majority**   **Right**

What's evident from this permutation is that the people at the extremes have something in common with each other that distinguishes them from others—their engagement with politics. On both the Left and the Right are the deeply committed, the news junkies, the activists, the tweeters, those who get emotion-ally invested in politics.

Political Polarization: An Integrate View

**Exhausted Majority
(Politically Disinterested)**

Left   Right

Deeply Committed

Less engaged in politics are people on the far side of the arc from both extremes. They might not be following the latest news developments—they likely have other priorities. Americans in this group are in the majority, and they are not interested in talk-ing with people on either end of the spectrum.

Aside from holding a skewed perception of the political spec-trum, we hold additional misunderstandings about the people on either side. Whereas we may think people in an opposing party don't share our principles, we're wrong about that. Around

90 percent of Democrats and Republicans value government accountability, fair application of laws, individual responsibility, and respect across differences, but only a third think the other party considers these important.[13] Furthermore, the vast majority of Americans value fair elections, integrity of public officials, and equal rights, yet people believe their own party values these democratic principles more than the other party.[14]

The Perception Gap

Let's say you like pie more than cake, but I think you *love* pie and *hate* cake. You have a preference for pie over cake, but it's not as strong as I think it is. The difference between your actual opinion and my assessment of your opinion is known as the perception gap.

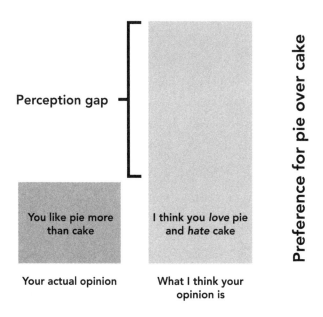

In terms of politics, this perception gap leads us to believe that most people are at either end of the political spectrum, even though studies show that the majority of Americans are in the middle.[15] This perception gap is widening, as partisans overestimate the ideological extremism and level of political engagement of people in the other party. Critics of unity echo these misperceptions as they express abhorrence at the idea of collaborating with extremists rather than envisioning the considerable population of moderates with more similar values.

Not only do we misperceive what people believe, but we also have distorted views of who people are. To a much greater extent than is actually true, Republicans think Democrats are queer, Black, godless union members, whereas Democrats think Republicans are old, rich, evangelical Southerners. Such perceptual biases tend to increase the more politically interested someone is.[16]

Another level of misconceptions about the other side has to do with your beliefs about what they think of you. Back to the pie versus cake example. You might think, because I'm a cake eater, I look down on people who like pie, even though I'm pretty accepting of those with pie preferences. Your belief about my opinion about your opinion is a metaperception.

Similar to the perception gap in assessments of opinions, these metaperceptions are also distorted. For example, one study showed Republicans images depicting the evolution of humans, from apes to *Homo sapiens*, and asked how evolved Democrats are on this scale. Republicans rated Democrats as more evolved than Democrats thought they would, and the same was true when Democrats rated Republicans. As much animosity as Democrats and Republicans have for each other, members of each political party think the level of dislike and dehumanization held by the other party is twice as high as it actually is. It also turns out that the more you think the other party holds prejudicial opinions about you, the more you want to distance yourself from them.[17]

One more thing. Do you have a picture in your head of Democrats and Republicans spouting off about politics? If so, you're not alone. We tend to radically overestimate how much partisans discuss politics, and we are loath to interact with these politically verbose Americans![18] Although we might think that affective polarization is driven by negativity toward political positions, in actuality, most people's negative feelings about people in either political party stem from simply not wanting to talk about politics.[19]

DEPOLARIZING

Are you fed up with divisive politics? Many Americans share this sentiment, with 70 percent seeing polarization as a barrier to solving major issues in our country.[20] Reflecting fondly on the past, people wonder how we became so polarized and how we can get out of it. They long for the days when they could engage in civil disagreements about politics. They recall that it didn't seem so hostile back then. They could disagree and still be friends.

As much as Americans want to overcome divisiveness, few are optimistic that the United States is heading in this direction.[21] The good news is that numerous individual, interpersonal, and institutional actions can reduce polarization.[22] In fact, correcting misperceptions is an effective depolarizing strategy. Just by reading these past few pages, you've made a difference.

To successfully depolarize, we'll need to grasp how we, as individuals, interact with structures of our society. In *Why We're Polarized*, journalist Ezra Klein contends that polarized political institutions exploit our identities: "Toxic systems compromise good individuals with ease. They do so not by demanding we betray our values but by enlisting our values such that we betray each other." Furthermore, our two-party system preys on our natural proclivity for dualistic thinking—reducing issues to dichotomies that amplify differences and cloak similarities.[23] These institutions capitalize on historical, cultural, racial, religious, ideological, and regional differences that have hardened into tribal identities.[24] Systems such as news and social media interact with cognitive biases to solidify and exacerbate polarization; however, there are actions you can take to control their input and impact.

KEY TAKEAWAYS

- Ideological polarization, differences of opinions about issues, has been present in our country since its founding and is not surprising in a healthy democracy.

- Affective polarization, animosity for people across the political spectrum, has increased dramatically and is having a detrimental impact on our communities and country.

- Tribalism is ingrained in humans and drives our responses to people in and outside our groups.

- We overestimate political polarization and misperceive who people on the other side are and what they think of us.

- Americans are eager to depolarize but not optimistic about the prospect of doing so, although there are many strategies that will support depolarization.

CHAPTER 2

Consume News Wisely

When I was growing up, my parents read two daily newspapers—the *Washington Post* and our local paper—listened to NPR in the morning, and watched the evening news. In between these activities, they didn't have additional updates on the news. They were very well informed via print, radio, and TV, but their news consumption was contained.

Back in the day, TV news came from the major networks, of which there were three: ABC, NBC, and CBS. Each network showed a range of programming: talk shows in the morning, soap operas in the afternoon, sitcoms and dramas in the evening, and Saturday morning cartoons. News was scheduled in the early evening before nighttime TV. According to the Federal Communications Commission's Fairness Doctrine, established in 1949, these broadcasters were required to cover controversial public-interest topics and to present diverse and opposing views.

This was not a perfect system. As much as a single narrative about the news meant we were all more or less on the same page in terms of factual information about current events, it was not a page that reflected everyone's perspective. There were certainly faces and voices and experiences underrepresented in the limited range of options. Nonetheless, broadcast news represented journalistic integrity, and most people felt they could trust what they heard from the newscasters.

Then came cable TV. I rejoiced in the opportunity to see music videos anytime I wanted rather than only on Friday nights. My mother enjoyed the ready availability of classic movies. And, suddenly, there were entire TV channels that showed news twenty-four hours each day.

The news channels first appeared as a boon. To participate in our democracy, people need to know about the issues and the candidates they're voting on, don't they? So, more information must be better, right? When Ted Turner founded the first twenty-four-hour news channel, CNN, in 1980, he hoped to create a more informed global public, articulating his vision that the network's coverage would "bring together in brotherhood and kindness and friendship and in peace the people of this nation and this world."[1]

Few would argue that Turner's original concept has come to fruition. Under pressure from a relentless news cycle and from competition with new networks like Fox and later the internet, twenty-four-hour news networks turned away from hard news to opinion-driven punditry. This shift to opinions and away from news resulted in the diminishment of fact-based journalism and turned the news channels into competing worlds, each of which caters to a particular perspective and is crafted to keep our attention. Meanwhile, the 1987 termination of the Fairness Doctrine opened the floodgates for one-sided AM talk radio shows. These shifting media outlets cultivated an audience that consumes large quantities of emotionally activating and narrowly focused content, all of which exacerbates political polarization.

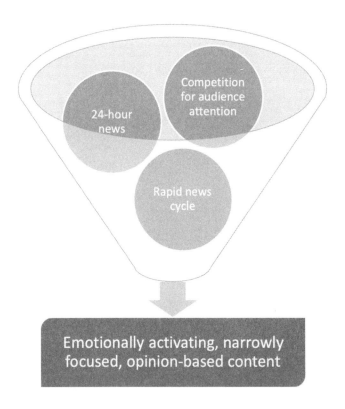

At the same time, sources for local news have been in steep decline. America loses more than two newspapers each week, especially in under-resourced counties, yielding increasingly larger news deserts.[2] Print, broadcast, and digital journalism are suffering financial woes that winnow news outlets and drive desperation for audience attention. Meanwhile, Americans are looking to social media, such as Twitter/X and Facebook, and increasingly TikTok, as a regular source of news.[3]

What's the role of the current news landscape in political polarization, and what can we do about it? Today's news interacts with polarization in various ways, through high volume, biased content, representation of political extremes, and problem-focus. Let's discuss how each aspect impacts political polarization, and strategies to help you consume news wisely.

VOLUME OF NEWS

Americans feel overwhelmed by the volume of news they are subjected to.[4] It reaches us through our TVs and radios and newspapers and apps and websites. Notifications pop up for everything from international conflict to partisan political battles to pop star divorces. Updates are constant, so if you look away, you may miss the latest about what's going on in courtroom testimony, the weather forecast, or a labor dispute.

The advent of twenty-four-hour news channels necessitated production of vast quantities of content. In addition to an increase in demand for traditional journalism, commentary fills more airtime. Pundits share opinions, make predictions, and spar with the opposition.

To maintain audience interest, it's advantageous to keep emotions activated. Getting us riled up is what sells: Humans get hooked by emotion, especially tribalism that pits us against an enemy. And news outlets collect data on what audiences respond to, a process considerably simplified by the internet compared to tracking TV and radio engagement. So, news has increased in volume, both in terms of amount and tone of content.

As cable channels offered choices in what news to watch, they have been able to cater to the views of their audience more narrowly. The more they focus on explaining why their viewers are right and the other side is wrong, the more their viewers engage.[5] People can consume news that supports their opinions and justifies their negativity toward others whose values, identities, or lifestyles differ from their own. You might assume that, with content catered to what the audience wants, consumers would be happy—validation in one's beliefs feels good, and news is a business built on selling emotional content. Yet, the public is largely dissatisfied with the news media, and trustworthiness in news sources has decreased over time.[6]

The increased volume of news and punditry also shifted the standards for being an informed consumer of news. For instance, the depth of one's understanding is no longer the barometer of how knowledgeable a person is, nor even is the breadth. Rather, the measures have become, can you spout an opinion, do you have a hot take, can you fire off a scathing critique of an opposing view? It seems like everyone has become a political commentator. We all feel like it's our job to be pundits: "I must have an opinion. I must weigh in."

It can feel satisfying to be an armchair pundit, to hear your views and values reflected and amplified by news commentators. Equipped with talking points, you can support your positions in conversations with family and friends. Furthermore, it feels important. You're not simply watching sitcoms or reality shows; you're also paying attention to significant events that have an impact on people's lives. Nonetheless, the way much of the news is structured keeps you overly engaged, emotionally activated, and viewing the world from an increasingly narrow vantage point.

Although it's important to be informed, it's not necessary for most people to stay on top of the news every minute. To loosen its grip on you, try turning off the news and disabling the notifications on your phone. Rather than keeping the news on in the background while you're doing other things, tune into the news for a predetermined length of time, and then turn it off and engage in other activities with your full attention. Regain control by using your remote control!

If you're a dedicated news junkie, know that your addiction is being fueled by increasingly unhealthy content—your news is laced with commentary, bias, and overemphasis on extremism. Consider harm reduction strategies to maintain your interest without unwittingly getting sucked into an endless stream of polarizing content. More about the impact of overexposure to that content follows.

POLARIZING BIAS

In fall 2021, there was ample coverage of the partisan divide in COVID vaccination rates. Indeed, the disparity was real; according to the Centers for Disease Control and Prevention COVID Data Tracker, 90 percent of Democrats had received at least one dose compared to 61 percent of Republicans as of late October 2021.[7] Nonetheless, there was a key fact that wasn't getting attention, which is that a majority of Republicans were at least partially vaccinated. This statistic was inconsistent with the media portrayals and mental images Democrats had of anti-vaxxers shunning public health directives, which, at most, was less than 8 percent of adults in the United States.

By highlighting the differences between Democrats and Republicans and ignoring the similarities, the news shapes behavior. Perceived norms impact our health choices, especially when there is strong affiliation with group identity. For example, college students who overestimate their peers' alcohol consumption tend to drink more than those with more accurate assessments.[8] Thus, perceptions of the number of vaccinated people in your own political party can play a role in your intent to get vaccinated. What if the news had highlighted how common it was for people of all political parties to get vaccinated rather than the conflicts about it? How might that have influenced actual vaccination rates, as well as the divisiveness over vaccinations?

Journalists mistakenly think of the general public as deeply involved in politics, overestimating ordinary people's affective polarization and political social media engagement.[9] This skew is evident in coverage of political conflict. It's not surprising that political polarization is compelling to journalists; compared to interviewees who have more nuanced opinions about politics, conflicts about extreme views likely make a more powerful story that garners views and clicks.

Take, for example, this experience. A well-respected journalist contacted me to see if I was doing any programs they could sit in on. Indeed, I was having a discussion the following evening for a college that had adopted *Beyond Your Bubble* for a campus read. It took some finagling to get permissions for a journalist to sit in, and to extract assurances from the journalist that attendees would have their confidentiality maintained to my satisfaction. I was excited for the journalist to hear how people were applying the skills from the book and to get a sense of the challenges and successes readers were experiencing as they attempted to engage in dialogue across political lines. Consistent with my prior experiences with people who had read the book, the attendees shared how helpful they found the skills; they felt better equipped and more optimistic than they had been previously. A few weeks later, the story came out. The journalist, or perhaps their editor, had chosen not to use the material from the campus program. Instead, the story featured a support group for family members of QAnon conspiracy theorists, who were feeling distressed and hopeless. Any empowerment these family members felt was based on limiting their expectations and interactions with their loved one.

It's not that this story wasn't accurate or wasn't important. It's just clear that it had a specific slant toward focusing on conflict due to extremism rather than optimism for connecting across the divide. Generally, the news is more likely to show us people who are on the extremes rather than those in the middle. Since 2008, there has been a considerable increase in news media references to extremist groups, especially those on the Right.[10] Some argue that focusing on extremist groups normalizes hate and lends them greater visibility.[11] In an attempt to expose the dangers of violent hate groups, journalists may have tapped into a "morbid fascination" that hooks their audience on this content.[12]

In addition to the focus on extremes, news media tends to emphasize polarization over cooperation. For example, the *New York Times* published 900 articles about political polarization in a seven-year period (2006–2013).[13] Although the vast majority of this coverage framed polarization as bad for policymaking, and most articles contained appeals for bipartisanship, less than half referenced actual examples of bipartisan behavior. So, although the *New York Times* did not explicitly encourage polarization, their emphasis was on highlighting polarization over reporting on cooperation across party lines.

News media distorts consumers' perceptions of the political divide by providing disproportionate coverage of people who are on the extremes and by overemphasizing polarization.[14] It's clear that most people are not reflected in the narrative of polarization between the Left and Right. Yet, polarization is what we hear about, and this media bias toward polarization fuels misperceptions and discord. In fact, the thing people on the Left and Right have in common is their distorted perception of each other. Democrats and Republicans think that the majority of people in the other party have extreme views, but in reality, only a minority, around 30 percent of either party, are on the furthest ends of the spectrum. Interestingly, the more centrist someone is, the more accurate their views are of people on either side, whereas those who consume polarizing media have more skewed perceptions.[15] So, we have people on the far Right imagining all Democrats as anarchists firebombing the Portland police station, while folks on the far Left are picturing anyone who voted for Trump as a tiki torch–bearing White Supremacist. But that's not what most people are like. In fact, you're a lot more likely to encounter someone with more centrist or mainstream views, even if they vote for or identify with a political party.

Americans recognize and fret about media bias, even in their go-to sources.[16] Nonetheless, news sources are producing content that consumers respond to, so we, the viewing public, are contributing to the problem. And that means we can also be part of the solution. What if we, as a country, lifted our view from screens that showcase people who are narrow, extreme, ignorant, and hateful? What if instead we became aware of the full range of people who may have a different perspective than we have, and what if we saw them as collaborators in developing a fuller picture of humanity? Maybe then, we could harness our collective power to solve the problems of our country, rather than buying into and participating in the overhyped narrative about division.

WHAT INFORMATION ARE WE EXPOSED TO?

Despite media biases, outright deceptive content comprises less than 1 percent of Americans' news consumption. On average, we interact with fake news less than one minute per day.[17] Nonetheless, misinformation, inaccurate statement of facts, disinformation, and intentionally misleading or false claims can affect health, voting, and violence.[18] Americans are very concerned about misinformation, viewing it as the greatest challenge posed by the media environment.[19]

Media Literacy

Whether or not the content aligns with our ideological stance, we're more likely to fall victim to fake news when we don't take the time to consider it carefully. Given the opportunity to reflect on headlines, people are able to spot falsities that they miss upon first glance.[20] Although we like the idea that we can trust our gut reaction, it turns out our intuition fails us when it comes to discerning truth from fiction. A second look and a moment of reflection can help align us with reality.

Media literacy steers us to inquire about the authorship, format, audience, content, and purpose of messages we encounter.[21] In other words, it's the practice of reading for the integrity of the content as much as for the data it presents. Analyzing and evaluating the information we're exposed to helps us sort out fact from fiction (more about how this relates to social media in Chapter 3). Even simply slowing down and carefully considering the veracity of the news you consume will help you to spot the more obvious misinformation.[22] You can also check websites such as the News Literacy Project (https://newslit.org/) or Snopes (https://www.snopes.com/) to fact-check stories that arouse your skepticism. Such strategies empower you to understand the context of news media and choose how you relate to it.

Small Slices of Information

In my view, an even more insidious driver of political polarization than misinformation is the small slices of information we consume. Even news outlets that are strongly grounded in facts are not showing the whole picture. Because we are choosing news sources that align with our views, and because it's impossible for any news source to cover every newsworthy event in the world, or even in our country, state, or community, we are each exposed to only a small slice of reality.

On January 6, 2021, when Trump supporters invaded the US Capitol, it was shocking. I had never seen anything like it, nor had most of my friends and family. Violent protesters targeted our federal government and attacked law enforcement officers who were bravely protecting our country. How could all Americans not be equally shaken? How could Republicans not see the threat to our democracy?

Mystified but curious, I started digging around to try to gain some insight into how reactions on January 6 could contrast so greatly. I discovered that, just days before the Capitol insurrection, there had been a violent riot in Portland. Months of rallies had led up to the New Year's incident in which protesters firebombed a federal courthouse building, set fires, and threw dangerous objects at police. I viewed footage of masked protesters hurling fire at police. It looked scary, like it could easily get out of control. I can point out a dozen obvious differences between the Portland riots and the January 6 insurrection. That's not the point. The point is that I had no idea the Portland riots had occurred. I started asking around. Had my Left-leaning friends seen the footage of the Portland riots? No, they hadn't. Or they had, but that was different.

Interestingly, the *New York Times*, one of the news sources that people on the Left find most credible,[23] had altered their coverage of the Portland protests in fall 2020. For example, a headline that originally stated, "Federal Officers in Portland Face Rising Opposition," later read, "Federal Officers Deployed in Portland Didn't Have Proper Training." As the paper's online news stories about the riots were updated, wording and perspective shifted to delegitimize police and morph protesters from troublemakers into righteous citizens.[24]

I wondered what the invasion of the Capitol would have looked like to me if I had been exposed to nightly footage of the Portland protests in the months leading up to it, including the violence only days before. I might have seen similarities in the chaos, the civilians embattled with police, the attack on federal property. I might have been befuddled by Democrats suddenly lauding law enforcement, seven months into the zenith of the Black Lives Matter movement and calls to defund the police.

Some viewers try to balance things out by watching the news produced by and for the other side of the political spectrum. People tell me they're trying to gain insight into those who consume this news or that they need to know what the opposition is saying in order to combat it. Although they report to me that diving into the opposition's news source further solidifies their views, one study found that Fox News watchers who were paid to watch CNN for a month demonstrated shifts in their knowledge and attitudes.[25] It's possible that the impact of watching the opposition's news depends on the mindset—are you relishing the biases and gaps that confirm your view of the other side as ignorant and ill informed, or are you seeking to gain an understanding of another viewpoint? Ultimately, it may not be as important to try to expose yourself to all the pieces of the pie as it is to recognize that you are consuming only one small slice and that other people are as well.

There are some excellent resources that can help you understand the news in the context of biases. One is All Sides (allsides. com), which seeks to offer balanced news and diverse perspectives. They provide media bias ratings of every piece they publish so that the reader will be aware of the author's or publication's viewpoint. Another resource is Ground News (https://ground. news/), which gathers content from thousands of news sources and makes it easy to decode what is being presented by media on various sides of the political spectrum. Reviewing these platforms offers an informative glimpse into what people may be exposed to, depending on their news source, and it can make you a more knowledgeable consumer of news media.

PROBLEM VS. SOLUTION FOCUS

I used to subscribe to *The Nation*. If you're not familiar with *The Nation*, it's an avowed progressive publication that was founded by abolitionists in the 1800s. I would read through the non-glossy pages of deeply researched, dense background and analysis of social and political ills. As a result, I was extremely well informed about the absolutely terrible state of our country, and I felt paralyzed by the magnitude and intricacies of the problems. How could I possibly tackle the myriad complex problems that faced our country? So, I did nothing to try to solve them.

Overwhelmed and depressed, I allowed issues of *The Nation* to pile up, eventually canceling my subscription. Seeking an alternative source of news, I discovered and subscribed to *Yes! A Journal of Positive Futures*. It published stories about what people were actually doing to improve the world. It provided adequate background that better informed me about the issues, and it felt so encouraging to read about actions people were taking.

It's not that we should avoid all negative media content; it doesn't benefit us individually or collectively to pretend that the problems of the world do not exist. Nor should we feed on a constant stream of suffering as the emotional overwhelm can have negative psychological consequences and short-circuit our willingness to help those in need.[26] We can, however, choose media that empowers as it informs rather than relying on shock, pity, or emotional activation. Restorative narrative is an approach that highlights how people recover from adversity. Rather than sensationalizing tragedy or offering false hope, restorative narrative covers complex journeys of resilience in the aftermath of violence, loss, and other significant challenges.[27] By cultivating empathic knowledge, these stories can even promote vicarious growth for the audience.[28] *Yes* is an example of a magazine composed of restorative narratives. Do you know of others? Perhaps when you discuss politics with friends and across the divide, you'll share them.

KEY TAKEAWAYS

- The current state of news media is overwhelming, biased, and emotionally activating.

- News media tends to overemphasize and overestimate extremism and polarization, and higher consumption leads to distorted perceptions of people on the other side of the political spectrum.

- Media literacy can help to combat misinformation and disinformation.

- You are almost certainly being exposed to only a small slice of reality that is different from the small slice that's being presented to people on the other side of the political spectrum.

- Consume news wisely by limiting your intake, approaching media with a process of inquiry, and exposing yourself to positive and solution-oriented news.

CHAPTER 3

Use Social Media Intentionally

Social media is trying to get your attention. Your phone bings—no, it's not your friend texting you. It's an alert that a comment or new post is available. You sense the immediacy and click to the source. You access the app and gobble up bite-sized, personalized content based on prior interactions. The infinite scroll function offers endless panda videos, analyses of Taylor Swift songs, and bisexual advocacy (or maybe that's just my feed). These features tap into human psychology and forge your actions into habits.

Like any organism or business, social media is doing the thing it needs for survival: keeping you engaged. With the proliferation of available content, digital products compete for your attention, which is a valuable commodity to advertisers. In this "attention economy," social media applies algorithms to maximize your time on their platforms. Their strategies include prioritizing content with the highest engagement potential, such as that which activates emotions, reinforces existing beliefs and biases, and expresses animosity toward opponents. In polarized times, social media can easily amplify political conflict.

Social media companies appear to be succeeding at hooking our attention, with the average American having seven social media accounts on which they spend over two hours per day, often while at work.[1] Among US adults, the most popular platforms drawing our attention in 2021 were YouTube (81 percent), Facebook (69 percent), and Instagram (40 percent), with about a quarter using Twitter/X and Snapchat.[2] TikTok's popularity is booming, now reaching 54 percent of adults,[3] who devote more time to watching these short videos than they spend on any other social media platform.[4]

Nonetheless, social media is a complex force in society. Even critics agree that, although features of social media may exacerbate conflict and partisan animosity, it is not the root cause of political polarization.[5] Furthermore, social media can have beneficial impacts related to social support, identity and meaning making, and task mastery.[6] For all of its attention-grabbing and contribution to polar slant, what if certain approaches to social media could actually turn down the volume on polarizing input?

SOCIAL MEDIA AND POLITICAL POLARIZATION

Not infrequently, I encounter someone who divulges that their attempt at dialogue across political lines was unsuccessful. When I ask for details about the conversation, they tell me they responded to a social media post that they disagreed with, and things went south from there. This provides me with an opportunity to clarify the definition of "conversation" and to suggest that dialogue should take place face-to-face, not Facebook-to-Facebook. There are some aspects of social media that render it a problematic forum for political discourse.

Let's Talk Tweets

Are you part of the 25 percent of Twitter/X users who produce 97 percent of the content? If so, you're probably mostly resharing or replying to posts rather than creating original content.[7] You're especially apt to reshare political content, which is almost twice as likely to be recycled compared to nonpolitical content.[8] And if you're tweeting a lot about politics, you're more likely to be politically engaged, attentive to the news, and extreme in your views compared to other Twitter/X users.[9] You're also consuming content that reflects your own views, and you loathe political adversaries.[10] Twice as likely to reference the opposing party than your own,[11] you intensify affective polarization by generating focus on opinions about the other side rather than opinions about the issues. Given these characteristics of frequent political tweeters/X-ers, the content on this platform distorts reality, leading the consumers to think that everyone is politically interested, engaged, and extreme.

When we see a social media post that we disagree with, we might think that sharing back some information, a link to a research article, or a logical argument supporting our own view will help the other person to be more knowledgeable about the issue and perhaps to recognize the errors in their thinking. Surely, sharing is caring, isn't it? It turns out, that's not what happens. To find out how people respond to contrary information on social media, I looked to a study of over 1,600 partisan Twitter/X users.[12] Researchers reshared liberal messages to Republicans and conservative messages to Democrats and found that not only did participants fail to come around to the other side, but they actually became more firmly committed to their original positions, even becoming more extreme in their views. Discord on social media can increase both the distance between opposing ideas and the animosity partisans have toward one another.[13]

Origins of Twitter/X Content

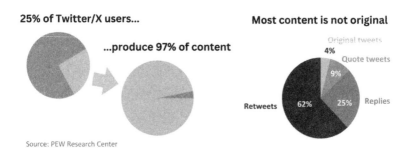

25% of Twitter/X users...

...produce 97% of content

Most content is not original

Original tweets 4%

Quote tweets 9%

Retweets 62%   25% Replies

Source: PEW Research Center

People who engage in political interactions on social media are generally hostile, both offline and online, and they gain visibility in social media environments.[14] Even if they're not the primary cause of political conflict, social media platforms intensify friction and falsehoods.[15] And given the ease of seeking and sharing information that's congruent with our existing beliefs, social media exacerbates political polarization by amplifying our biases.[16]

Making Choices

We may be drawn in by social media for entertainment, connection, and information. However, the negative side effects become apparent when we stop using it. Look at what happened when Facebook users deactivated their accounts for a month prior to the 2020 election: They engaged in more offline social and solitary activities, they paid less attention to and knew less about political news, and they became less polarized. Their psychological well-being even improved.[17]

What if the problem isn't the nature of social media platforms, but rather how we choose to interact with them? Recently, researchers tried changing Facebook algorithms to see if these formulas drive polarization on social media. They found that modifying the Facebook feed didn't affect polarizing attitudes, trust, or knowledge, suggesting that the divisive impact of social media may rest in users' hands rather than in what Facebook feeds us.[18]

Another study demonstrated the power of choices we make on Facebook. Users were presented with news outlets that contrasted with their views, and they could choose whether or not to interact with them. When they did access these sources, it didn't change their opinions about the issues, but it did make them less hostile toward people who held differing views.[19] These findings show that if we engage with news that conflicts with our perspective, we will not be brainwashed, but we may gain some insight into the reasoning of people on the other side. Moreover, we don't need to wait for social media to change the algorithms. We can simply subscribe to a few news outlets outside our bubble (see allsides.com to identify the political leaning of various news sources). Self-determination is a powerful force that reminds us we are not at the mercy of the machines.

Despite its inadequacy as a forum for dialogue, social media has some beneficial uses for combating political polarization. I sometimes consult Twitter/X to get a sense of what people on different sides of an issue are saying about it. Seeing the range of views associated with a single hashtag offers insight into multiple perspectives on a topic. I'm not alone in doing so. Whereas frequent tweeters/X-ers are more likely to express their opinions rather than to be exposed to those of other people, infrequent tweeters/X-ers are more likely than active users to say they use the platform to stay informed and see different points of view.[20]

We're in the best position to gain insight when we're intentional in our approach to opposing views on social media. Try remembering what it's like to have a disagreement with a friend before you dive into content that reflects a different political perspective than your own. This will put you in a less adversarial frame of mind.[21]

It's encouraging to know that over half of Americans, across party affiliation, say they have changed the way they use social media to be less divisive and more constructive.[22] With their swift changes to culture and communication, it's easy to blame big tech algorithms and twenty-four-hour news for a polarized nation. But ultimately, human decisions and actions may play a more significant role in polarization than aspects of social media platforms that are out of the user's control. In the end, we choose who we follow and friend, what we share and repost, and how much time we spend doomscrolling or watching TikTok dances.

HOW MISINFORMATION SPREADS

In 2019, a story kept popping up in my Facebook feed about Tanya McDowell, a Black woman who had gone to prison for lying about where she lived so her child could attend a better school. Her situation was juxtaposed with Felicity Huffman and other celebrities who had paid to get their kids into prestigious schools. My friends posted the original story to demonstrate the lack of parity in how a poor Black woman was treated in comparison to wealthy, famous White parents. Indeed, it did seem biased and unfair. Most of the comments expressed outrage at the injustice, and I was feeling it, too. There was one comment that stood out from the others. It said simply, "That's not the whole story."

The comment piqued my curiosity and sent me to Snopes, a site I use to check the veracity of questionable information. There was, indeed, an analysis of the situation. McDowell was a mother who was sentenced to five years for a combination of crimes, including the school district one, but also several more serious crimes, and it was not her first offense. Snopes confirmed these facts, along with Huffman's fourteen-day sentence. Although recognizing inequities in the criminal justice system, they deemed the comparison to be a poor one.

To be sure, knowing more details about the story did not quell my overall concerns about disparities in the US educational and justice systems, but it did temper my fury about this particular situation. It also kept me from hitting the "share" button and promoting a skewed version of the facts. When advocates provide only part of the story, it's all too easy for their message to be dismissed and their credibility called into question by people who don't share their views and, additionally, have been exposed to more information about the case.

People who post on social media can either create their own content or they can share posts from other accounts. Generating original content requires a degree of reflection that reposting does not. Due to the ease of resharing content, it is more apt to spread inaccurate or distorted information. Just as it's easier to believe repeated information as true in offline circles, we may regard reposted misinformation online as accurate, especially when we receive information from a source we trust or have a personal connection with.[23] Pausing to consider the veracity of information helps to diminish spreading misinformation.

You know what's not particularly great at curbing the spread of misinformation on its own? Being human. It turns out that psychologically, we are prepared to accept misinformation that supports what we already believe to be true. (This is called *confirmation bias*, something we'll discuss more in Chapter 4.) We're even more likely to embrace unverified information if it helps us make sense of a crisis, and we're particularly apt to spread misinformation if we are feeling anxious.[24] In addition, sharing misinformation is socially reinforced; our social media network engages enthusiastically with questionable, juicy content, whereas they turn away when we refrain from sharing such posts, which reduces our influence.[25]

All of that said, once we're aware of ourselves and our state, we can take steps to identify misinformation and keep from sharing it. Think twice before sharing distressing content, unconfirmed reports, or posts from unknown accounts.[26] It might be helpful to think of the acronym SIFT: Stop, Investigate the source, Find better coverage, and Trace claims, quotes, and media to their original context.[27] Social media literacy is a little different from mass media literacy (described in Chapter 2) because we can all contribute to content. So, we may need to do some self-reflection about what we're putting into, as well as what we're

The SIFT Method

Steps you can take to identify misinformation and keep from sharing it.

S **top**

I **nvestigate the source**

F **ind better coverage**

T **race claims, quotes, & media to their original context**

Source: Van Kampen (2023)

getting out of, the platforms.[28] Ideally, the more of us who apply these strategies, the less polarizing input will show up in everyone's social media feeds.

BUILDING A HEALTHY RELATIONSHIP WITH YOUR PHONE

As the sun set on a Friday evening, I set my phone to "do not disturb," which meant the only people who could reach me were my mother's caregivers. I plugged in my phone and put it down for the weekend. As I made dinner that evening, there were no podcasters keeping me company, no NPR reporters having me consider all things, no audiobooks being read to me by their authors. As I sat down to eat, I could not witness my friends' meals via Facebook and Instagram; I couldn't see what was trending on Twitter. It was very, very quiet.

This was fall 2020, and I was participating in a three-month Buddhist program that included several cloistered weekends. This program occurred early in the pandemic, so I joined the teaching sessions via Zoom from my home, where I lived alone. To foster introspection and practice, boundaries for the cloistered weekends included silence, no internet or media, and turning off my phone. Wait, what? Turn off my phone? For two whole days?

The first few hours of phone detox was the hardest. Every few minutes, I felt the impulse to reach for my phone—to text a friend, to check the weather, to glimpse social media. I recognized with dismay that the most significant relationship I had in my life might be with my phone.

When you rearrange the letters of the word "listen," it spells "silent." In the calm of cloister, I realized that this applied not only to listening to other people, but also to myself. As the thoughts and feelings that get kicked up settled, I felt a sense of calm relaxation. With external quietude, my inner guidance was more apparent and could lead me to simple decisions, like what to eat, as well as more fraught ones, such as how to respond to someone attacking my beliefs or identity.

Yes, social media can be distracting and addictive, but it's not the only way that we're keeping our minds busy and our emotions activated. In the United States, 85 percent of adults own a smartphone,[29] which we use for a wide variety of purposes, the least of which is talking on the phone. You might use your phone as an information source; entertainment in the form of music, videos, podcasts; a camera; and a way of staying connected to

other people. Often the things we're doing on our phones feel productive—listening to a book, managing email, tracking our exercise. Nonetheless, they churn up our minds and draw us into a myriad of apps every time we pull out our phone.

I'm not suggesting you get rid of your phone altogether, but perhaps try developing a more intentional relationship with it. In *Log Off: Self-Help for the Extremely Online*, Sammy Nickalls recommends increasing awareness of technology use and creating digital boundaries (for example, charging your phone away from your bed), and investing in activities and connections outside the digital world. If you're looking for structured guidance, Catherine Price outlines a monthlong, day-by-day plan in *How to Break Up with Your Phone*.

Writing this chapter inspired me to experiment with some changes in my phone use. I set up a charging station near my front door so I can plug in my phone when I enter rather than carrying it around with me in my home. I silence my phone when I want to focus on what I'm doing or the people I'm with. I designated the hot tub a "no phone zone." Just by wearing a watch when I go out, I notice I don't look at my phone as much. When I'm waiting for a friend or a bus or the light to change or when my dining partner goes to the restroom, I try resisting the temptation to pull out my phone. Even taking a pause before I reach for my phone interrupts automatic behavior and helps me change my habits.[30] By implementing these actions, I feel like I have more control over my phone rather than vice versa.

I've learned that whatever I'm using my phone for can wait. I can wait to see what politician said something provocative. I can wait to satisfy my curiosity about which picture won the Oscar in 1966. I can even wait to respond to a text from a friend. There may be some drawbacks of not being connected to my phone constantly—my daily step count will not include those I take while doing laundry, I might miss the opportunity to play pickleball that day, I might need to do math in my head, I might be caught in the rain—but the benefits of quieting my mind, being fully present with myself and others, and exerting free will more than make up for these inconveniences.

TAKING CONTROL OF SOCIAL MEDIA USE

When I started researching this chapter, I assumed I would find overwhelming evidence for the evils of social media, tempered by a few specific uses that were beneficial. I was surprised to learn that, when taking into account data from hundreds of studies, social media had a fairly insignificant association with psychological well-being, with small effects on both positive (e.g., social well-being) and negative (e.g., anxiety and depression) indicators.[31] Even the impact of social media on adolescents varies based on the user's characteristics and how they interact with various functions of the platforms.[32]

When it comes to politics, social media promoted free speech and organizing that toppled authoritarian regimes in the Arab Spring—and it also has the potential to aggravate partisan rancor that threatens democracy.[33] Similarly, although social media is often the vehicle for spreading scientific inaccuracies that can damage individual and collective health, researchers can use these platforms to disseminate research findings to the broader public and to correct misinformation.[34] Social media is a tool that can be used for many purposes with both detrimental and beneficial consequences for individuals and society. Most important, we each have the power to determine our relationship with social media. Control of smartphone use is literally in our own hands. To regain control . . .

- Establish boundaries to keep your attention focused where you choose rather than being directed by the platform.

- Turn off notifications for all social media apps.

- Set a time limit when you do tune in to social media.

- Set an intention for what you want to get out of it.

If you need to take a mental break from work, just watch one video; you're less likely to lose hours of your day than if you swipe to the next and next and next.[35] You can also make use of the features in the apps or on your phone or computer that alert you to excessive social media engagement. The Center for Humane Technology (humanetech.com) offers additional guidance regarding healthy use of technology, such as reducing use of distracting or deceptive apps, eliminating clickbait, creating tech-free spaces, and engaging in a digital detox.[36]

Social media can help to create a sense of community, especially when you don't have a local network of people who share your cultural or religious background, sexual orientation or gender identity, or interests (scholarly, creative, sports, etc.). I love being connected to other writers, learning about a colleague's recent publication, and sharing knowledge about bisexuality or listening skills. I also enjoy the personal connections—seeing friends' children dressed up for Halloween, rediscovering my best friend from fifth grade, celebrating my friends' personal and professional accomplishments. Also, like many other Swifties, TikTok taught me how to make friendship bracelets in preparation for the Eras Tour. When we use social media to strengthen our connections to others rather than to create divisions, we have the best opportunity to use technology to support our health, our relationships, and our social fabric.

KEY TAKEAWAYS

- Social media is designed to maximize user engagement.

- Although social media isn't the root cause of political polarization, it can exacerbate hostility.

- Address misinformation on social media by recognizing and not spreading it.

- Take control of your digital media usage by being intentional about your phone usage and changing automatic habits.

- Build healthy relationships and community, both online and offline.

CHAPTER 4

Correct Distorted Perceptions

"Snowflakes," "fascists," "racists," or "those crazy idiots." No
matter what side you're coming from, these terms may come to
mind as you imagine connecting with folks on the other end of
the political spectrum. These perceptions are fueled by the media
and social media representations we've discussed in the previous
chapters. But there's another source of polarizing input—our
own minds.

PREJUDICE

Are you prejudiced? It's a loaded word. You may balk at the question, at the implication that you might prejudge someone based
on what they look like or a group they belong to. If you are aware

that prejudice contributes to mistreatment, discrimination, even ethnic cleansing, you certainly would not want to embrace this scourge. You probably distance yourself from thinking of yourself as prejudiced and consider people who are to be irrational, biased, and malevolent.

Given the negativity you likely feel about prejudice, I hate to break it to you that you are unquestionably prejudiced. In fact, we all are. It's a characteristic of the human mind to understand people based on categories. Every moment, we are bombarded with an inconceivable amount of information through our senses—we receive data through sight, sounds, tastes, smells, and physical sensations. There is no possible way we can give full attention to the entirety of this input on a granular level, so our minds employ shortcuts.[1] We pay attention to familiar cues and fill in the gaps. This helps us make sense of a complex world and satisfies a basic evolutionary need to conserve mental processing resources for survival needs.

How does this play out in the context of politics? Let's say you are politically Left-leaning, and you meet someone at a social gathering who says they're a Republican. Your mind immediately pulls together information about the concept of "Republican" based on previous experience, but also on what you've heard in the news and social media. You might conjure up images of people chanting "lock her up," the January 6 invasion of the US Capitol, and bans against diversity training and gender-affirming care for transgender people. Now, you're thinking about this person as if they're aligned with all these pieces of data—a MAGA hat–wearing insurrectionist who agrees with everything touted by commentators on Fox News. But, for all you know, they could be a moderate Republican who disavows the idea that Trump won the 2020 election. Similarly, if you lean Right, you might imagine all Democrats to be social justice warriors who are firebombing police stations and undermining family values, even if they are married with children and have never attended a protest. Once your mind has created a picture of who this person is, it will take considerable effort and evidence to overcome.

Although all human brains are wired for prejudice to some extent, there is some individual variation. Some people are driven to resolve ambiguity and seek quick and definitive answers—they need "cognitive closure." People with a high need for cognitive closure tend to view things from a single perspective and associate specific characteristics with groups of people, a key aspect of prejudice.[2] Before you jump too quickly to judge them as less evolved, keep in mind that these people also do well on IQ tests and computational speed. They are smart in a way that helps with pattern recognition, but that may also lead them to rely on mental shortcuts associated with prejudice.[3]

In contrast to people who need cognitive closure are those interested in understanding the root of other people's behavior and considering many different possible causes for it. This quality of "attributional complexity" makes people less likely to rely on prejudice and more likely to be viewed by others as empathic, thoughtful, and socially wise.[4] It's helpful to know which is a stronger pull for you—resolving ambiguity or looking at human behavior from many perspectives. If you're a star at pattern recognition, be on the lookout for your own prejudice.

Despite the evolutionary benefits of identifying people by categories, this way of thinking limits us. We reduce people to a narrow set of characteristics that may not be accurate, and we miss out on understanding the fullness and complexity of other humans. Moreover, prejudice about people on the other side of the political spectrum contributes to interpersonal conflict and societal polarization. That Republican you met at the party may be a potential friend, ally, or business contact that you might dismiss due to prejudice.

COGNITIVE BIASES

Prejudice reveals that the human mind contains some flaws in its operating system. These cognitive biases have the effect of distorting our perceptions and interpretations of ourselves and other people. Several of these biases have considerable impact on political division: confirmation bias, naïve realism, and motive attribution asymmetry.

In my TEDx Talk, "What Halibut Fajitas Taught Me about Bridging the Political Divide," I shared a story that revealed my cognitive biases. This was a true story about a situation in which I got very sick after eating halibut fajitas, and because I assumed I had food poisoning, I ignored the symptoms of appendicitis, an almost deadly error. Let's take a look at how cognitive bias influenced my thinking and put me at risk.

When I told my friend Laury about my stomachache, I was sure it was food poisoning because I had just eaten halibut fajitas. Because Laury had gone through an appendectomy, she floated the possibility that it might be appendicitis. I immediately rejected the notion because the pain was in the middle rather than on the right side of my abdomen. I kept focusing on the fact that I had eaten halibut fajitas right before getting sick, and I dismissed the idea that it might be appendicitis. Although, when I finally Googled "appendicitis symptoms," it turned out that I had all of them. I had fallen victim to confirmation bias.

Confirmation bias steers us to focus on information that supports what we already believe to be true and avoid or dismiss information that contradicts our existing beliefs.[5] This bias narrows our view by directing our efforts toward confirming our position. As a society, our awareness of confirmation bias has increased over the past few years. You may be familiar with the idea that disparate news sources, social media feeds, and politicians shape how we perceive things, even what we accept as facts. As we've come to recognize our political bubbles, understanding confirmation bias helps us make sense of beliefs that are anathema to our own—how someone can buy into QAnon, or how people can think we should defund the police. Confirmation bias helps explain why some people are certain gender is binary while others are confident it isn't. There's a more widespread recognition of the impact of confirmation bias . . . on other people, but it's so much harder to see it in ourselves. People who rant about the biased news that's shaping the views of those idiots on the other side are convinced that their own news source is unbiased, and that their outlook is the correct one. As humans, we are loath to acknowledge that our own perceptions may not be fully informed.

Clearly, I did not want to admit that my self-diagnosis of food poisoning might not be the correct one. In fact, I doubled down on my certainty because I had acted on my beliefs. Not only had I barked at Laury and excused myself from dinner due to food poisoning, but I had also conveyed the information to the restaurant, who had, for all I know, thrown out their entire supply of halibut based on my accusation. (Side note: I did call the restaurant from the ER to tell them I was mistaken, and they were very nice about it.) It turns out, taking a stand puts us in a psychological mindset that's resistant to change. By expressing our convictions forcefully or otherwise behaving in ways that are consistent with our beliefs, we effectively persuade ourselves. So the more we voice or vote our position on an issue, the greater our unconscious motivation to stick to it.

Not only did I not want to admit that Laury might be right about appendicitis, but I questioned her reasoning as well. I brushed aside her concerns, thinking "she's such a worrier," rather than honoring her credibility as a scholar with expertise in women's health. Whereas we are very adept at persuading ourselves, we are likely to reject someone else's attempts to change our minds. Due to another cognitive bias, naïve realism, we believe our own interpretations are objective and logical while others' analyses are skewed by emotion, self-interest, and ideology.[6] So when we encounter people whose positions contradict the information we've been exposed to, we see them not only as uninformed, but also as irrational zealots, which makes it easy to dismiss them. Naïve realism helps to explain why I saw Laury's concern as a character flaw.

Although I assessed my friend as well intentioned, it is not uncommon to see our motivations as benevolent and our opponents' as hostile, even hateful.[7] This bias, called "motive attribution asymmetry," can feel very satisfying because it maintains your conviction that you are right, as well as fosters a sense of moral superiority. You are not only correct in your opinions; you are also a smart and good person in contrast to the heartless, ignorant, and unprincipled people on the other side. To consider a different perspective as valid may threaten your denigration of your opponents, and consequently your elevation of yourself.

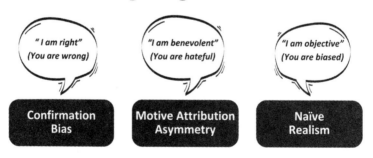

Polarizing Cognitive Biases

"I am right"
(You are wrong)

"I am benevolent"
(You are hateful)

"I am objective"
(You are biased)

Confirmation Bias

Motive Attribution Asymmetry

Naïve Realism

The consequence of our cognitive biases is that we tend to think people on "the other side" of the divide are extreme in their views, uninformed or misinformed, irrational, and immoral.

Given our distorted views of people across the political spectrum, it's surprising that we would want to interact with them at all, and indeed, you might find yourself trying to avoid these folks altogether. Fortunately, despite my demonstration of cognitive biases, Laury and I remain friends. In fact, she drove me to the hospital for my appendectomy, took care of my cat, picked me up the next day, and never once said, "I told you so." I aspire to Laury's grace.

WHY CORRECT OUR MISPERCEPTIONS?

Why might we want to correct our misperceptions? Clearly, when we rely on distorted understandings of other people, we're wrong a lot of the time, and when we express these misperceptions about others, it makes us a little foolish. We are buying into what media, social media, and cognitive biases feed us rather than forming an accurate view of reality. This also diminishes our credibility with people who do see things more accurately. My cousin married an Israeli who was raised in a liberal family. Benny heard from his family about how people on the political Right were uninformed and hateful. When he entered his mandatory military service and met people from a range of political persuasions, he recognized that his fellow soldiers on the Right were smart and kind and brave. This changed his view about people on the Right, but it also discredited people on the Left who disparaged them and left him feeling ashamed of the view he previously held of his compatriots. By framing the opposition in narrow terms, we may lose political allies who share our values, but who dislike our bigotry toward our adversaries.

In addition to having a more accurate perception of other people, we may want to correct our misperceptions because they affect our behavior in ways we may not feel good about if we recognize the flaws in our assumptions. Because we misjudge people as more extreme than they are and view them as uninformed and uncaring, we may shun and unfriend people due to distorted understandings of who they are. We also may avoid political dialogue or enter into it with assumptions about others that undermine our approach. Ultimately, cognitive bias damages our connections with other people, and we need these relationships to support our psychological well-being.

Cognitive distortions don't just affect our interpersonal behaviors, but they have implications for our democracy as well. Studies confirm that the vast majority of both Democrats and Republicans value foundations of democracy, such as free and fair elections. However, people in both parties believe that the other side is much more willing to violate democratic norms than their own side is.[8] Particularly concerning is that when we believe the other side is supportive of antidemocratic activities, we are more likely to violate democratic norms ourselves. This is also true of metaperceptions, what we think others think of us. The more we overestimate the other side's prejudice toward us, the more willing we are to breach democratic norms to the advantage of our own party.[9]

So, correcting our distorted perceptions will help us see other people with greater accuracy, which will reduce our prejudiced thinking and behavior, help us stay connected with other people, and strengthen our democracy.

HOW TO CORRECT OUR MISPERCEPTIONS

When you're driving, you can see what's in front of you by looking forward, and there are mirrors to check what's behind you, but you may still be missing something. We call the areas out of view a "blind spot" or "dead angle." These visual limitations can be dangerous because we lack awareness of other drivers, which can lead to a collision.

Remedies for our visual limitations as a driver consist of awareness, prevention, and compensation. The first step is to be aware that there may be areas around the car that are outside your visual perception and to know when it's most important to attend to these areas (e.g., when turning a corner or changing lanes). There are ways of adjusting the rearview and side mirrors to broaden the driver's view as much as possible. Finally, drivers can turn their head briefly while driving to check the areas out of their line of sight.

How does driving relate to cognitive bias? In both cases, there is something outside our perception that limits our understanding and might lead to negative outcomes. What might be out of our awareness when we encounter people we perceive to be different from ourselves or who we assume are similar to us? How might we apply remedies of awareness, prevention, and compensation to correct our distorted perceptions?

Awareness

Awareness of our blind spots, of cognitive bias, can help to prevent negative outcomes. Our minds typically operate without our awareness of what they're doing. Understanding that cognitive biases exist and how they affect our thinking can help to correct distortions. If you've gotten this far in the chapter, you likely have a sense of the existence and consequences of these biases, so you're well on your way! There are a few additional variations in how biases operate that will be helpful to consider as well.

All cars have some areas out of the driver's sight line, but some vehicle designs have larger dead angles than others. Similarly, although cognitive distortions are characteristic of all humans, there is individual variation among people's susceptibility to bias. Do you want to quickly zero in on an answer, or do you seek out multiple ways of viewing things? Knowing whether you tend more toward cognitive closure or attributional complexity will help you assess how difficult it may be for you to challenge your biases. Knowing yourself is an important component of the change process.

Prevention

Prevention entails broadening your view to bring more potential obstacles into your perceptive field. As far as cognitive bias goes, this entails combating the tendency to arrive quickly at narrow conclusions about people unlike ourselves and consider a wider range of possibilities about who they are, what they believe, and what motivates them.

One effective way to shift your bias is to expose yourself to data about people on the other side of the political spectrum. There's an impressive project called the Strengthening Democracy Challenge that invited researchers to develop activities to reduce partisan animosity. Of 252 interventions submitted, they tested 25, 23 of which reduced negative feelings toward people in the other political party. One of the mechanisms of change they identified was simply correcting misinformation about people in the opposing party. As you've come to see in this section, there is a great deal of data that refutes our misperceptions of people on either side of the political spectrum. Keep this information in mind to correct your distorted thinking or try the online activities developed in the Strengthening Democracy Challenge.[10]

You might also implement mental strategies to counter your own narrow views. For example, try acting as a debater for a perspective you disagree with. As a member of their debate team, generate logical, well-supported arguments for their point of view. You can also go on the offense by trying to poke holes in your own reasoning. In dialogue across disagreement, I suggest we encourage elaboration as it will help people recognize the limitations of their own understanding. Similarly, you can provoke your own curiosity by trying to fully articulate in a step-by-step manner how your ideas would work.

Remember that the human mind is likely to focus on limited cues and fill in the gaps with generalized, and often biased, information. Thus, it's important to recognize when you are jumping to conclusions about what someone believes. A stance, a slogan, or even a pronoun is taken to mean a vast array of positions and values and morality. If I say, "Black lives matter," and you say, "All lives matter," we might be quick to assume we know the entirety of each other's belief system. Noticing the mental picture you create about someone based on limited information can interrupt our automatic assumptions and make room for a more complete and complex picture.

Adam Grant, author of *Think Again: The Power of Knowing What You Don't Know*, recommends enlisting other people as a "challenge network." These are people you can ask to help broaden your view and point out the limitations in your thinking. A vital characteristic of this network is that there is a sense of psychological safety with these people, so choose them with this in mind. According to Grant, they can be an effective learning community only if you know they will not degrade or poke fun at you.

Compensation

A fellow psychologist, Jill Lee-Barber, encourages people to "check your blind spot" when thinking about other people. What is the equivalent of checking your blind spot when it comes to cognitive bias? When you are driving and you want to make sure there is nothing out of your view, you must shift out of your comfort zone, lean forward a bit. You must also turn your head to take your eyes off your ultimate goal in order to assure you are not doing damage in the journey to get there. Challenging your cognitive biases can create discomfort, and you may feel like it derails you from your drive for certainty, but ultimately it will benefit you.

If we return to the driving metaphor, there are some special circumstances to consider. The risk related to limited vision is compounded under certain driving conditions, such as darkness and rain. Similarly, you may be most susceptible to cognitive bias when you feel threatened or anxious. Thus, it's important to be aware of your emotional state, learn how to regain equilibrium, and seek out opportunities to challenge your biases in settings that offer psychological safety.

When driving, there are some situations where visual limitations may particularly endanger someone else; bicyclists and motorcyclists are especially vulnerable in collisions. Cognitive bias may also be particularly harmful in some situations. When you are in a position of power over someone else, you have more potential to do harm. For example, if you have authority in hiring or promotion decisions, your biases can have an economic and professional impact on others. It's also important to be vigilant about cognitive bias if your prejudice can do physical harm to others.

Even those with a high need for cognitive closure, who are more likely to fall into prejudice, are amenable to shifting their view through intergroup contact.[11] When we're feeling anxious, as we often are when encountering people who are unfamiliar, we're likely to rely on negative prejudice. However, when we have positive interactions with people across the political spectrum, our anxiety decreases, and we latch on to their agreeable characteristics, which can counteract our prejudiced tendencies.

AWARENESS

Assess your susceptibility to cognitive bias

PREVENTION

Broaden your view about other people: who they are, what they believe, and what motivates them

COMPENSATION

Shift out of your comfort zone by challenging your cognitive biases

OVERCOMING RESISTANCE TO CORRECTING MISPERCEPTIONS

Even though there are negative consequences of bias for our accurate comprehension of others, our relationships, and our democracy, you will likely resist correcting these distortions. I wouldn't be surprised if you reject being characterized as prejudiced and consequently push back against the implication that expanding your perspective may be beneficial. You might even accept that cognitive biases exist, but you think the other side is more susceptible than you are. This might reflect naïve realism at work, making you think you are more reasonable than those who disagree with you. It is characteristic of the human mind to inflate other people's biases and minimize our own. If you're thinking, *Other people are prejudiced, but I'm not,* please keep in mind that there is a substantial body of research demonstrating cognitive distortions across party lines. If you believe in science, but you don't believe in *this* science, confirmation bias may be clouding your view.

Beyond the role of cognitive biases themselves maintaining cognitive biases, what else might be going on? Cognitive biases may support our motivation to see ourselves in a particular way. Do you like the idea that you are smarter than people who disagree with you? Do you want to think of yourself as kind in contrast to the other side's malevolence? Does it feel satisfying to believe you are more reasonable than they are? A colleague jokingly responded to a presentation I did with, "Are you telling me I need to give up my self-righteousness?!" We might have the sense that disparaging others' beliefs maintains our superiority. Removing the distorted lens of cognitive bias may leave us in a less positive light—not necessarily inferior to the other side, but not superior either.

Perhaps our biases help us justify our outrage or our behaviors. If we cut off family members, post snarky memes, or relocate to an area with like-minded neighbors, we may have a hard time laying down our bias. We have a drive to resolve cognitive dissonance, conflicts between our behavior and what we think is right. If our behavior is out of alignment with more accurate views of the other side, we may hang on to our distorted understanding of them that supports our actions.

There's no question that we can benefit from correcting our misperceptions. Even so, it may also be important to acknowledge and accommodate the reasons that we cling to them, as Shankar Vedantam and Bill Mesler explain in their book, *Useful Delusions: The Power & Paradox of the Self-Deceiving Brain.* Fear and ambiguity threaten our sense of security and stimulate prejudice as a means to strengthen our tribal bonds. Since prejudice is activated by a sense of being threatened, it may be helpful to increase awareness of our underlying feelings of vulnerability. If we're able to attend to our fears more directly, perhaps we can diminish our reliance on prejudice as a way to comfort ourselves.

To be sure, people can be uncaring, and political beliefs can arise from aggression. Nonetheless, our cognitive biases steer us to view people outside our own group through an overly negative rather than overly positive lens. When we expand our view to consider a broader range of possible motivations, we may not conclude that our adversaries are saints. Challenging our beliefs does not mean we should ignore violence and hate speech; in fact, this process entails deeper examination of our political opponents rather than turning away and relying on mental distortions.

So, what's the payoff to viewing our adversaries with greater accuracy? A shift in perspective can turn down the dial on stress about political conflict. Feeling less embattled, we are more likely to maintain relationships with loved ones who have opposing views. Optimism will encourage us to stay engaged across political differences. In short, challenging our biases can sustain our most cherished assets: health, human connection, and democracy.

KEY TAKEAWAYS

- Humans are wired for prejudice. Paying attention to familiar cues and filling in gaps helps manage overwhelming input from a complex world. It does not, however, help us to view others accurately.

- Confirmation bias, naïve realism, and motive attribution asymmetry lead us to see people who disagree with us as uninformed, illogical, and hostile.

- Due to cognitive biases, we tend to think of people across the political spectrum as extreme, different from us, hateful toward us, and willing to benefit themselves at the cost of democracy.

- We can correct biases using awareness (knowing our tendency to rely on prejudice), prevention (accurate information, mental strategies, and external supports), and compensation (applying additional effort in particularly challenging circumstances).

- We are likely to resist changing our views of people on the other side, but doing so will benefit us individually, in our connections with other people, and as a society.

Building Individual Capacity

Let's pause for a moment. That is, in fact, what I've been suggesting you do in each chapter so far. Pause before you assume your slice of the news is the whole story. Pause before you reach for your phone. Pause on the verge of making a judgment about someone on the other side of the political spectrum.

As you pause now, take a moment to reflect on where you are in the process of navigating a politically polarized society. You likely started this journey with particular ideas about the people involved in political conflict. You might have seen yourself on one side or the other, or perhaps you were more of an observer, watching the two sides duke it out. Either way, this might be a good time to reflect on how your experience may be shifting.

Now that we've explored how news, social media, and our own brains have distorted our views of ourselves and people on the other side of the divide, are there assumptions that you have discarded or that you want to challenge? Knowing that your understanding of the political and human landscape was likely limited and skewed, do you hold the same hopes, goals, and fears that you did when you started reading this book? Having turned down the volume on polarizing input, do you have more space to reflect rather than react, to build rather than battle? What will it take for you to move forward confidently into a changed perception of reality?

In addition to making space for reflection, pausing can help us break habitual patterns. Did any of the behaviors described in Part I resonate with you, and have you tried making any changes to reduce polarizing input? Where are you in the journey of consuming news wisely, using social media intentionally, and correcting your misperceptions? If you're not where you want to be yet, try identifying some goals based on the material in Part I that you can put into practice.

As you move forward into the next few chapters, there will be more opportunities to embrace change. Part I of this book focused on turning down the volume of polarizing input. Part II is about what we need to build up in ourselves. How do we cultivate our individual capacity to face the fracture of a politically divided nation?

For me, this portion of the journey brings to mind the story of *Moana*, a Disney movie that depicts a Polynesian girl finding her role as a leader among her people. ***Spoilers for Moana*** She sets out across the sea, determined to subdue the malicious demigod Maui, and to demand that he return the stolen heart to the goddess Te Fiti, which will restore abundance to Moana's village. Along the way, Moana discovers that what she learned about Maui from the legends was not the full story. He did not steal the heart out of maliciousness; he was seeking love and appreciation. Understanding his true motives softens Moana toward Maui; she gains humility and empathy as she sees things from his perspective. They both drop their facades, share their vulnerabilities with each other, and become allies, working together to save Moana's village.

Moana faces a series of challenges, each of which makes her more capable of navigating rough seas and finding her way amid uncertainty. When she faces a crisis of self-doubt, her connection to her family and ancestors restores her faith in herself. In her final challenge against the volcanic demon, Te Ka, Moana recognizes it as the goddess Te Fiti underneath her fury. Rather than fearing Te Ka's wrath, Moana welcomes contact and restores the heart, transforming demon back into goddess, thus healing the world. The lesson conveyed is that Te Fiti is not defined by a stolen heart and that she knows her true self.

The story of Moana reminds us who we truly are. Beneath the hubris, the anger, the tales of enemies, we are all connected and generative and bravehearted. And this knowledge frees Moana and her people to be their authentic selves. Part II of this book will equip you to shed qualities that do not serve you and to reveal your true self—capable, curious, and compassionate.

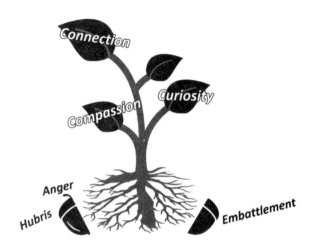

The coming chapters attend to body, mind, and heart. Resilience is largely about managing the body's response to threat, rendering us more adept at facing challenges. Opening your mind is facilitated with the quality of intellectual humility and strategies like perspective taking. Empathy and compassion are the tools of your heart. Fortifying these dimensions of yourself will strengthen your internal capacity to navigate political polarization and will help you in other areas of your life as well.

One more pearl of wisdom from *Moana* before we move forward. I looked into the cultural accuracy of the story and learned that, historically, Polynesian people explored the seas, but that they stopped for 2,000 years before they returned to seafaring. And this period is known as "the Long Pause."[1] They were explorers, but for a long time, they stayed put on islands. Possibly due to toxic conditions that made their island environments unsustainable, they set sail again. Perhaps we have been isolating ourselves on islands that have become uninhabitable due to toxicity of political polarization. Maybe it's time for us to set sail beyond the comfort of our political islands.

There will be more pauses in the chapters that follow—pauses before emotional reactions, pauses before you assume what another person thinks, pauses before you turn away from your adversaries or wish them ill. Pauses that interrupt habits and make space for empowerment. But for now, let's end our pause, and hit "play."

CHAPTER 5

Foster Emotional Resilience

Let's say you're on the political Right. Leaving your home, you see a neighbor's lawn sign demanding a lengthy list of political stances as a requirement of crossing their threshold. You log on to a Zoom meeting, and everyone has their pronouns indicated with their names. At the gym, the person working out next to you is wearing a "Black Lives Matter" T-shirt.

On the other hand, perhaps you're Left-leaning, and you notice a pickup truck in your neighborhood with an NRA sticker. You pass a billboard that reads, "Protect the Babies. Choose Life." You go for a walk and pass someone wearing a red baseball cap.

Or perhaps you're in the middle, like most people, part of the exhausted majority. Politics is not your main priority, and you are tired of hearing the vitriol. Yet, throughout your day, you encounter bold headlines about indictments, strangers striking up conversations about politicians, relatives ranting about people on the other side.

No matter where you stand on the political spectrum, you are likely exposed to environmental cues that trigger your emotions. Sometimes you may see cues as indicators of differences, or, at worst, as mild irritants. But in the ongoing context of political division, you may experience such meaning-filled symbols as threats to your values, your identities, your freedom, even your existence. When we perceive threat, our body kicks into action. A chain reaction starts in the amygdala, a part of our brain that senses danger, which signals the hypothalamus to stimulate the sympathetic function of the autonomic nervous system, which causes the endocrine system to release hormones.[1] In a split second, this response happens outside of your awareness, but it causes noticeable physiological reactions, including increased heart rate, rapid breathing, flush, and muscle tension. The body is preparing to act in the face

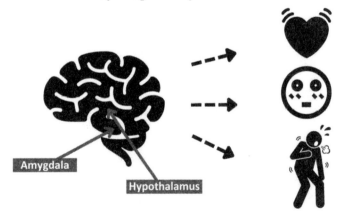

Physiological Response to Threat

Amygdala

Hypothalamus

of danger. It is calling on your physical resources to engage in battle (fight) or get away from the threat (flight).

The body's fight-or-flight response is designed to protect us from danger, and it is beneficial when we're faced with an acute threat. Our body kicks into gear so we can respond effectively to a tiger, a bear, or a shark. After the danger has passed, our parasympathetic nervous system takes over and returns our bodies to normal functioning. We regain equilibrium.

But what happens when, instead of a tiger, a bear, or a shark, we repeatedly encounter bumper stickers, billboards, and social media posts? This type of ongoing activation short-circuits our stress response cycle. The stress switch remains in the "on" position, leaking stress hormones into our bodies, keeping us at a heightened state of activation and inflaming tissues. This type of chronic exposure to stress can increase risk for health problems such as cardiovascular disease, autoimmune conditions, and depression.[2] Indeed, political polarization contributes to stress on many levels—physiological, psychological, interpersonal, and collective.[3]

Americans are feeling strained by political conflict, with two-thirds citing the current political climate as a significant source of stress in their lives.[4] But how has political division in the United States become a persistent driver of anxiety, fear, and pain? As our political identities morph into tribal divisions, we peer across the political spectrum with mistrust. Not only do we view the other side as extreme and irrational; we also perceive them to be hostile toward us. We see them as threatening pivotal freedoms and wanting to do us harm. No wonder politics feels scary, especially when you feel like your values are not represented by those in public office. For example, during the Trump administration, politics took a significant toll on a range of health markers—everything from stress, loss of sleep, or suicidal thoughts to an inability to stop thinking about politics and making intemperate social media posts. These effects were particularly pronounced for those on the political Left.[5]

While there are indeed egregious acts carried out by a few emboldened actors, they are not the norm. How do we steady ourselves when news and our minds collude to instill fear? It may be helpful to recognize that our very reactivity is often being used against us. Meaning, the other side provokes for the sake of getting a rise out of people on our side as a weapon of political battles. The strategy to aggravate liberals, or "own the libs," drives some of the focus on the culture wars.[6] Meanwhile, the Left tightens the reins on "deplorable" conservatives through diversity policies, pronoun use, and pandemic mask wearing.

In Part I of this book, we learned about ways to turn down the volume of polarizing input. Limiting input from news, social media, and cognitive distortions helps our bodies to maintain equilibrium and likely makes us less reactive when we encounter environmental triggers. These strategies may not, however, completely eliminate all discomfort related to political polarization. You will probably find that particular events in your country, community, or daily life increase your stress levels.

The stressful climate of political polarization presents us with many challenges. We can respond to those challenges in a variety of ways, some of which build internal resources that strengthen our ability to bounce back from adversity. We call this successful adaptation to difficult life experiences "resilience." Less beneficial responses to environmental challenges of political polarization further entrench us in psychological and interpersonal strife. Before we dive into how to build resilience, we'll look at some of these common ways people respond to political polarization that are *not* aligned with resilience.

COMMON MANIFESTATIONS OF POLITICAL STRESS

If you're like most people, resilience is not your go-to response to political stress. Most people are more likely to fall into outlooks and behaviors that increase distress. Here's where we get ready to take a deep breath and look at ourselves gently but with a frankness required for introspection. Ready? Let's consider three common ways that stress manifests in the context of political polarization:

- Avoidance

- Victim mentality

- Aggression

Notice if you recognize yourself in these profiles. If so, do you perhaps bristle at how I've framed them? I want to assure you that I present these without judgment. My aim is to equip you with knowledge that may help you consider your default mode from a new angle. I include them here because, even while they are common and understandable, there are shortcomings associated with each that may not be readily apparent. It's important that you're in a position to make an informed choice about how you respond to political stress, so here we are, chatting about our lesser natures. But in keeping with the promise of building resilience, following this section, you will find guidance for ways to approach political stress with intention and empowerment.

Avoidance

Perhaps you've noticed that politics is increasing your stress, so you've been keeping your head down and trying to stay out of the fray. You block childhood friends on social media, skip family gatherings, and remain silent when coworkers start talking about their opinions on current events. Nonetheless, you're aware that politics is on your mind and that you feel tense every time you dodge people and activities that might contain political content or conflict. You may try to disengage from the problem by distracting yourself or having a few drinks.

It's not surprising that people try to avoid stressful situations. When you don't feel capable of facing the threat in some satisfactory way, focusing on it is likely to increase your distress and anxiety.[7] A friend told me she hadn't read my book *Beyond Your Bubble* because she was afraid she would actually have to have a conversation with people on the other side of the political divide. She was not only avoiding the interactions, but even shying away from a resource that would better equip her to be successful in them.

It turns out, attempting to completely avoid stress is not a helpful strategy. By giving yourself the message that you can't handle the situation, you undermine your ability to take action. You assiduously avoid experiences that could make a difference, and you miss opportunities to do something to alter the situation. Moreover, you cultivate the mindset that you cannot do anything to ameliorate your circumstances. Even if you think you can handle it but simply don't want to, you pass up experiences that could promote understanding and repair relationships. Although you may choose to opt out of potentially problematic situations at times, overreliance on avoidance and distraction are not adaptive. In fact, these coping strategies are associated with feelings of helplessness.[8]

What if a situation isn't just unpleasant, but actually seems dangerous? Isn't avoidance the best thing to do under these circumstances? Indeed, exempting yourself from physical or severe psychological damage is adaptive; it's important to keep yourself safe. I notice, though, that sometimes situations feel perilous when people are uneasy but are not genuinely unsafe. When our mental images of political adversaries are distorted due to political polarization, we may perceive greater threat than is truly present. Correcting distortions (Chapter 4) will help to address this problem, but it may not be sufficient to accurately assess and respond to perceived threat.

You might wonder what to do when the perceived threat brings up feelings related to past trauma. It's certainly natural to want to avoid memories and physiological responses associated with disturbing or painful experiences. Nonetheless, avoidance shouldn't be the only available strategy. The fact is, there is no form of therapy that recommends avoidance as a path toward healing, even for trauma survivors. Although within a trauma-informed care setting it is important to build trust and safety, the goal is to promote adaptive coping, not to learn to evade all triggers in the real world.[9] Ultimately, overreliance on avoidance is not a healthy strategy.

If this strikes a chord with you, if avoiding political stress is your default response, don't worry. You'll learn later in the chapter how you can face stressful situations with intention and skill.

Victim Mentality

Both sides of the political spectrum have a tendency to emphasize the other's power and their own vulnerability, even as they taunt the other side for their fragility. For example, people on the Right may feel like the government is coming after them and that Donald Trump is being persecuted, and they deride people on the Left as easily offended "snowflakes." People on the Left might laud their own support for marginalized groups, and fear gun-toting Republicans; they post pictures of Ruby Bridges, the first Black child to integrate an elementary school in the South (and who was pelted with rocks and slurs) along with, "If this child was strong enough to survive it, your child is strong enough to learn about it."

Vulnerability is a natural, human experience, and your awareness of feeling vulnerable is a strength. Especially if you have experienced trauma, you may be particularly attuned to environmental threats. Vulnerability may play out in specific ways in the context of political polarization. Perhaps you feel like the other side is powerful and your side is at risk. You may be concerned that rights that protect you are at risk. You might witness news of violent extremists on the other side, and you fear for your safety.

But what if you don't simply feel vulnerable in certain situations, but rather you typically see yourself as a victim across circumstances? This more ingrained pattern constitutes a victim mentality, which is associated with a lack of empathy, intensive focus on symptoms and causes of distress rather than solutions, and the tendency to elevate one's own morality despite treating others unfairly.[10]

Attention to the victim mentality is not intended to downplay the reality of victimization and trauma. You may recognize similarities between trauma survivors and people who hold a victim mentality. However, not everyone who experiences a deeply distressing and disturbing event has a victim mentality, and not everyone who sees themselves as a victim has been targeted. Viewing oneself as a victim in a particular situation is not a problem—it's preoccupation with victimization that's cause for concern.

The stakes are raised even higher when people are preoccupied with victimization, not of themselves as individuals, but of their political tribe. Perceived victimhood is associated with support for violence.[11] The more people focus on past victimization of their group, the less guilt they feel about doing harm toward another group and the less empathy they feel toward the other side.[12] A group victim mentality also impedes people's willingness to acknowledge atrocities committed by their own group against others.[13]

Many people who invaded the US Capitol on January 6, 2021, felt like the election was stolen by a powerful system that was not looking out for their interests. They saw President Trump as a victim, which justified the violence and havoc they wreaked that day. In the United States, politically motivated violent acts by people on the Left are less common and less deadly than those committed by people on the Right.[14] Nonetheless, activists protesting police brutality, capitalism, animal treatment, and environmental abuses may feel justified in employing aggressive tactics.

Feelings of group victimization are widespread. Most Americans (64 percent) feel like their rights are under attack. This statistic isn't just driven by a few select groups. When you break it down by population, over 60 percent of women and men, adults with a disability and those without one, LGBTQ and non-LGBTQ people, and Black and White Americans feel their rights are under attack.[15]

Why do people tend to frame themselves as victim, vulnerable, and attacked, and the opposition as powerful? Why wouldn't we want to own our power? One explanation has to do with recognition of structural inequities. There is ample evidence that

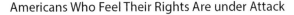

Americans Who Feel Their Rights Are under Attack

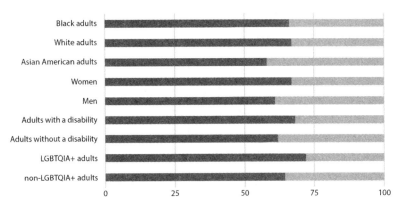

systems in the United States do not operate as an even playing field.[16] People of color, people with limited resources, people with disabilities, LGBTQ people, and others face structural and interpersonal stigma. If police stop and question you or worse, because residents thought your Black skin didn't look like it belonged in their neighborhood, if you were sexually harassed at work as a woman, if you were teased about wearing the only clothes your parents could afford, you might be painfully aware of racism, sexism, and classism.

One aspect of privilege is the ability to remain unaware of systems of oppression that benefit you. I do not have to notice when there is no curb cut in the sidewalk because I am not trying to navigate it using a wheelchair. I can be blissfully ignorant of gender restrictive restrooms because my identity and appearance are consistent with other people's expectations of where I should pee. It is easier for us to embrace ways in which we struggle due to aspects of our identities than it is to acknowledge benefits that we receive due to privilege.[17] Thus, we are all more likely to see ourselves as victims of the systems of our society than beneficiaries of them.

As we know from Spider-Man, "with great power comes great responsibility." People may also believe the converse, with disempowerment comes an absence of responsibility. Perhaps seeing ourselves as defenseless to a formidable foe relieves us of obligation to act, to acknowledge our role in a problem, or even to have empathy for those who may have been harmed.

Some people brandish their victimization prominently to limit exposure to environmental cues that challenge their identities, values, and ways of thinking. Some White people on the political Right do not want their children learning about the horrors of slavery because they do not want them to feel bad. Some college students on the political Left balk at free expression of views they disagree with from peers and campus speakers. Both sides attempt to limit the speech of their adversaries by limiting resources, establishing communication norms, and publicly criticizing people who do not fall in line with their approach.

Keep in mind that wearing vulnerability as protective armor does not equate to being truly vulnerable. You may have put on the armor to protect yourself, perhaps against a force that was dangerous at the time but is now a phantom enemy. But the metal suit no longer serves you—it weighs you down, renders you less nimble, obstructs your view. It may be time to shed the armor, to make yourself vulnerable, to reveal your true self.

Again, some people are truly victimized, and some groups are more targeted than others. It is not acknowledgment of the fact of victimization, but rather the preoccupation with it, especially on a group level, that finds synergy with political polarization. A victim *mentality* limits our empathy, disempowers us, and contributes to violence. Fortunately, there are ways of shifting our mindset that may offer paths to more adaptive responses. More about this later in the chapter.

Aggression

When we perceive threat, our body's natural "fight" response can manifest as aggression. You want to yell at your cousin or your neighbor or the TV. You are furious at the tactics of the other side. You argue in your head with politicians or news commentators. These types of venting can feel very satisfying. You get to channel your anger, release your feelings, and say whatever you want. Isn't that authentic, expressive, and emotionally aware?

Anger is a natural response to threat, and it can be channeled productively through assertive communication about one's needs. In contrast, hostile displays of anger may induce momentary positive feelings, but in the long run, they actually exacerbate aggression. Venting increases blood pressure in anxiety-provoking situations or when the recipient of the anger might retaliate. Furthermore, anger doesn't dissipate when you displace it onto a substitute target. Research participants who released their anger through physical activity (e.g., pounding nails, playing football, hitting a punching bag) demonstrated an increase in hostility. When people vent anger on a regular basis, it keeps them focused on aggression and becomes a habitual response to stress.[18]

Sometimes we are angry on behalf of others. This type of hostility may be particularly prominent in advocacy efforts for people who are vulnerable, like children. Both pro-life advocates and gun control advocates who are fighting for children's lives are angry. People who are fighting for gender-affirming care and those who are trying to protect children from sexual abuse are angry. Also angry are people who try to make sure the children in their community have adequate resources and those who attend to the needs of immigrant children.

There's a slogan: "If you're not outraged, you're not paying attention." This saying implies that, if you noticed injustices and injuries, you would unquestionably respond with anger. Moreover, absence of outrage might seem cold, uncaring, heartless, even mean. But is outrage the appropriate litmus test for paying attention, and is it the tool we want to use to motivate and embody advocacy? There are certainly ways in which outrage can be beneficial to express solidarity and motivate action. However, pervasive outrage may not be as helpful, and can even undermine your efforts that extend beyond your current circle of influence, who see things differently, who do not already view you as their moral compass. Specifically, outrage is not particularly beneficial for understanding or persuading others, finding common ground, maintaining relationships, and recruiting moderates. Without these functions, advocacy is limited only to activity among supporters. So, chronic outrage has limitations. It also can take a toll.

If you don't know how to shift out of an aggressive stance, prolonged outrage can have negative impacts. Outrage damages movements—if you are in a constant state of outrage, it weakens your credibility, even among supporters. Outrage damages your relationships—exposure to someone else's outrage can be abrasive, even if you agree with that person. Outrage damages your health—stress related to politics has been elevated in our country for the past several years, and this isn't good for our bodies. So, outrage can be helpful for some aspects of advocacy, but not good for others, and prolonged outrage can take a toll.

People tell me they're tired of feeling outraged, but it doesn't feel acceptable to stop. When we normalize outrage as the only acceptable expression of caring about a situation, we limit our options. Although occasional outrage may help you rally the troops, you can be an even more effective advocate, and you'll live longer, if you're not outraged all the time and if you have more tools. So, I want to encourage you to broaden your skill set (for example, see Chapter 8 for guidance on engaging across the divide). Because if you want your advocacy efforts to be successful and your personal relationships to sustain, outrage alone will not get you there.

If anger isn't further stoked, the feeling should dissipate on its own,[19] and the strategies in Part I can help you quiet sources of provocation. In addition, there are actions you can take to turn down hostility and channel your energy in positive ways. Read on to learn more!

Common Manifestation of Political Stress and Their Consequences

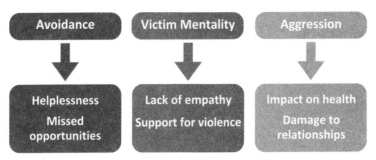

STRATEGIES TO FOSTER RESILIENCE

Given the body's natural response to stress, what role can we play in the outcomes? In fact, we are not simply at the mercy of our stress response. We also can influence it. The profiles previously described—avoidance, victim mentality, and aggression—reinforce negative emotions, helplessness, and long-term physiological and psychological problems. Other options strengthen our emotional capacity to withstand and make positive use of stress activation.

Managing Emotions

You've learned that political polarization may activate your stress response. You've also learned that, although venting emotion may feel satisfying in the moment, it is more likely to exacerbate than alleviate strong feelings. Ruminating on negative emotions is associated with depression and helplessness,[20] so it's not an effective strategy in the long run. What can you do with your emotions that will support your health as you navigate political polarization? What if you weren't so triggered in the first place? What if you could see a Black Lives Matter T-shirt or a Make America Great Again hat and not respond as a bull to a matador's red cape? It's not the environmental cues themselves, but rather the meaning you associate with them that kicks the stress response cycle into gear. Ideally, what you learned in Part I of this book will help you see people on the other side in more accurate ways, which may lessen your stress when interacting with them or messages associated with them. Reappraising the circumstances may help to reduce your reactivity.[21]

What if your emotions are already in high gear? What can you do to regain equilibrium? You can employ strategies that turn off the threat switch by engaging your body's parasympathetic nervous system. Deep breathing and muscle relaxation are simple techniques with measurable benefits for stress reduction.[22] Both behavioral strategies can be practiced when not under stress so you're prepared for stressful moments. Instructions for deep breathing and progressive muscle relaxation are plentiful on the internet, including videos on YouTube and TikTok. A great example is Dr. Andrew Weil explaining his 4-7-8 breath. I suggest you check out this and other options so you can find what you are most likely to put into practice.

Although exercise might feel like it revs you up more than it chills you out, physical activity can help you deal with stress.

Exercise offers a break from stressors, and twenty to thirty minutes of aerobic exercise can induce a calming effect that lasts for hours.[23] Furthermore, regular exercise can be helpful in reversing the damage of exposure to chronic stress.[24]

Simply being aware of your emotions without trying to change them promotes health as well. Mindfulness offers a means of remaining present and aware without getting jostled about by thoughts and feelings. It is a form of active observation of moment-by-moment experience, without trying to change what's happening. Mindfulness can be very effective at regulating emotions and consequently buffering the body from negative effects of stress.[25]

Emotional acceptance is a commonly used strategy that consists of being aware of and open to emotions without trying to alter or control them. Although distracting yourself from political stress and telling yourself it's not so bad can help you feel better, emotional acceptance uniquely promotes psychological well-being without dampening motivation to take action,[26] so this strategy may be particularly appealing to activists.

People sometimes balk at the suggestion they should calm their feelings when they're angry. They want to hang on to their righteous anger. They don't want their tone to be policed. It's important to note that tone policing is about managing our feelings for the benefit of others. Emotion regulation is about managing our feelings for the benefit of ourselves. Breathing, muscle relaxation, and emotional acceptance can offer immediate and lasting health benefits.

Seeking Social Support

Have you ever reached out to a friend when you're feeling agitated? If so, you may have noticed a calming effect from their presence. Even if people can't do anything to change an upsetting experience, social support can reduce the impact of potentially stressful or even traumatic situations.[27] When people are isolated, they're more reactive to stress,[28] whereas feelings of connectedness can lessen physiological response to threat.[29]

How can we make the best use of social support? In terms of political stress, rather than expressing hostility toward someone who doesn't share your values, try sharing your frustration with someone who is aligned with or can at least tolerate your viewpoint. Even in these conversations, it's not ideal to continue stoking the flames of aggression by venting with a compatriot who keeps you amped up through their own reactivity. The ideal use of social support is giving voice to strong emotion in a supportive setting, especially with someone who can help you gain insight.[30] Phone a friend who helps you feel more grounded as you release your emotions rather than one whose response fuels your anger spiral.

Harnessing Stress (Rising to a Challenge)

I do a lot of public speaking, an activity people fear more than death! It's certainly not relaxing to command the attention of hundreds of people, but the stress I experience doesn't impede my performance. In fact, it energizes me and helps me deliver an engaging talk. By viewing this stressful situation as a challenge rather than a threat, I'm able to make the best use of my physiological response to stress, which is designed to prepare me for challenges.[31] Similar to an athlete preparing for a game, stress can shift us into a high-performance mode![32]

What happens if we frame political polarization as a challenge rather than a threat? Can we harness the energy to embrace opportunities? For example, stress is most beneficial when we harness it to benefit our values and goals.[33] Political stress might bring attention to something meaningful in your life. Perhaps you notice that your blood pressure seems to rise every time someone mentions abortion. This might be a message to you that this is something you care a great deal about. Channeling your energy into posting on social media might feel like you're taking action, but as you read in Chapter 3, it has limited positive impact and greater potential to increase stress. Instead, consider taking action to support people who are being impacted by an issue you care about. For example, volunteer at a reproductive health clinic or a crisis pregnancy center.

Reaching out and supporting others is a type of response to stress known as "tend and befriend."[34] In the context of political polarization, it might be easy to respond to stress through connection to like-minded people. As you reach out, consider doing so in such a way that promotes nurturance of your people rather than combat against the enemy.

When I meet someone whose political perspective is different from my own, I'm excited to practice my skills and learn about their views. Interpreting my physiological response as enthusiasm rather than stress puts me in a mindset that increases the likelihood of a positive experience and decreases negative impact of activating situations.[35]

Flexible Coping

We've learned in this chapter that viewing stress as a challenge is adaptive, and chronic avoidance can be harmful. Are there ever times when you should opt out of a stressful situation or conversation? I asked my friend Linda Croyle, a healer and educator, when we should protect/distance ourselves from distress, and when we should get comfortable with it. She responded immediately, "Aside from truly dangerous or toxic situations, you can't leave until you can stay; you can't stay until you can leave." She credited her mentor, Dr. Sue Morter, with this wisdom. When Linda was struggling with her job and thinking about quitting, Dr. Sue gave her this advice, which encouraged Linda to look within to create a better work situation for herself and leave a few years later to pursue other interests, rather than to run from what she perceived to be an unsatisfying/challenging situation.

"You can't leave until you can stay; you can't stay until you can leave." What does this mean in terms of resilience in the context of political polarization? Basically, we need to develop the skills required to take an active role in coping with the challenges before us, we need to have the skills to opt out at times, and we need to have a sense of when to take each path. What we want is to have a range of options in our toolbox and choose the best one for the circumstances. Approaching each situation in exactly the same way is unlikely to lead to satisfying results. It's not that one approach is superior; rather flexibility is the key. In fact, researchers call this approach "flexible emotion regulation."[36]

Any particular strategy for coping with political stress is neither a magic cure nor a downfall. The key is flexibility. The most adaptive response to trauma is a flexibility sequence that involves assessing the context, applying various strategies in your coping repertoire, and making adjustments as needed.[37] Let's apply this approach to a politically charged situation.

Let's say your supervisor at work often expresses opinions about politics that are very different from your own. You have not shared your views, and you're concerned that doing so may have negative repercussions. Which contextual clues might be helpful to pay attention to? Consider the following questions:

- To what extent does your supervisor determine meaningful aspects of your work, such as pay, promotions, job responsibilities, and workplace atmosphere?

- What's the current status of your relationship with your supervisor? Do you generally get along, or is there some tension?

- What evidence is there regarding your supervisor's fairness or abuse of power?

- How much control do you have over the situation?

In addition to external aspects of the context, you might want to take aspects of yourself into consideration. Assessing your internal context may include examining your dispositions, trauma history, and culture. Your sensitivity as an adult may even have its origins in what you were like as an infant. For instance, some babies are highly reactive and not easily soothed; they cry a lot and are hyperaware of environmental stimuli—sounds, lights, temperature, even emotions of people around them. Depending how parents and others respond to infant temperament, these children may learn to soothe themselves or they may grow up to be particularly sensitive adults. Thus, the sensitivity of our physiological response to stress can vary due to heredity, as well as major stress experienced during one's lifetime.

There's also some evidence that our cultural background makes a difference in how we cope most effectively. For example, concealing feelings can have a negative impact for people from cultures that value self-expression. However, if you're from a relational tradition that prioritizes harmony, such as Asian societies, suppressing emotions is culturally congruent and not detrimental.[38]

Nature and nurture interact, leading to varied capacities for awareness of emotion and for withstanding distress. The goal is not for everyone to achieve a specific level of resilience. It is for everyone to reach their full capacity.

Taking this knowledge of yourself and the external context into account, how might you address the situation at work with your supervisor? In this chapter, we've discussed a range of responses to stress, including avoidance, venting, feeling victimized, managing emotions, seeking support, and rising to the challenge. Assess the resources and tools at your disposal. It's helpful to develop the skills you want to have in your repertoire, and if you haven't done so already, you can use your workplace stress as an opportunity to do so. For example, if you notice your body feels tense at work, try practicing progressive muscle relaxation.

Some strategies will be better for some contexts. For example, the more control you have, the greater your ability to cope with the situation by taking external action. When a situation is beyond your control, focusing on your reaction to the situation is more beneficial.[39] As you try various approaches, pay attention to how they're working for you. Monitor your internal feelings, as well as relevant aspects of your workplace environment.

Noticing the impact of your strategies will help you to make corrective adjustments, to try different approaches or fine-tune your skills. Let's say you try progressive muscle relaxation, and you find that it has some limited benefit, but you notice that you're still preoccupied with your supervisor's political diatribe. Perhaps you attempt to avoid your supervisor, but you recognize this is affecting your ability to communicate effectively regarding work. Maybe you try shifting your mindset to see this as an opportunity to rise to the challenge of expressing your needs assertively in the workplace. You seek support from friends who help you express your fears and practice what you want to say. At your next meeting with your supervisor, you say, "I've noticed when politics comes up in the workplace, it distracts me from my work. I know people respect you, so would you be willing to model not bringing up politics at work?" Your supervisor seems caught off guard, but you notice they don't make comments about politics anymore, and you find yourself more relaxed at work.

When I teach classes that contain difficult material, especially about sexual assault, I preface my lecture with the following guidance: The material we're about to cover can feel challenging—women often feel vulnerable, and men often feel blamed. Whether or not these describe exactly what's going on for you, I encourage you to pay attention to your response to the material. If you feel overwhelmed by emotion and need to step out, feel free to do so. If, however, you feel some discomfort, but you are able to remain engaged, I hope you will try sticking it out and using this as a learning opportunity.

My guidance regarding stress related to politics is similar to what I tell my students. Overall, I suggest you limit chronic exposure to stress (e.g., news and social media), opt in to facing challenges when possible, and harness your body's stress response toward meaningful action.

Strategies to Foster Resilience

 Flexible Coping   **Seek Social Support**

 Harness Stress   **Manage Emotions**

GROWTH

Each experience of stress offers an opportunity to further develop healthy habits in dealing with it.[40] As we rewire our systems to reduce maladaptive reactivity, embrace flexible coping, and adopt a positive mindset toward stress, we equip ourselves for life challenges.

Not only does political stress offer the opportunity to develop resilience, to regain our prior level of functioning after adversity, it may even confer additional benefit.[41] Following even the worst circumstances, some people find that their struggles yield positive outcomes, even when accompanied by stress. Hardships sometimes help us to identify priorities, make meaning of life experiences, and increase our repertoire of coping skills, resulting in post-traumatic growth.

The stressors we face in a divided nation may ultimately strengthen us individually and as a society. We can learn how to develop a healthy relationship with the proliferation of news and social media that has emerged in the past decade. We can develop interpersonal skills that help us navigate conflict and provide support. We can broaden our minds and open our hearts. We can build stronger communities and a more robust democracy.

You are taking this opportunity to learn about resilience, to develop healthy patterns, to cultivate skills. You are why I have hope that people can not only learn to survive politically polarized times, but also that collectively we will be better off having embraced opportunities for learning and growth.

KEY TAKEAWAYS

- Political polarization shows up in many aspects of our environment, and political stress is damaging our health.

- Avoidance, victim mentality, and aggression are common responses to political stress that are not helpful in the long run.

- Adaptive responses to political stress are managing emotions, seeking social support, and embracing stress to motivate action.

- Flexible coping consists of assessing the situation, identifying available resources and tools, and monitoring outcomes.

- Political polarization offers an opportunity to culti-vate mindsets, knowledge, and skills that can help us to flourish individually and collectively.

CHAPTER 6

Broaden Your Mind

You learned in Chapter 4 to correct distorted thinking. This will help you have a clearer perception of yourself and others in a politically polarized environment. But what about the issues? Is there something we need to do differently in our way of thinking about positions we and others take?

I suggested in Chapter 2 that any single news source exposes us to only a limited view of reality, one slice of the whole picture. How should we relate to all the other slices? If we're committed to our positions and don't want to reconsider them, is there any benefit in understanding another point of view, in digesting more than one slice?

When we see things only from our own view, we can be bewildered by the other side. People tell me all the time, "I don't understand how people can think or act or vote as they do." I used to think this meant, "I want to understand," but more often, it's stated with a tone of righteous conviction as if the lack of comprehension is a badge of honor, as if to say, "I am so moral, so informed, so correct that I cannot possibly fathom how someone could see things a different way." And so, we hold up our ignorance as a virtue, but truly, it is not only a personal shortcoming, but it also *disempowers* us.

People tell me they want to reach across the divide to persuade, find common ground, maintain important relationships, or gain insight. To achieve any of these goals, it's helpful to understand where another person is coming from, to know what their slice is like. Comprehending only a single perspective disempowers us by limiting our ability to achieve our interpersonal and advocacy goals.

So, what's the antidote? How do we broaden our minds? Intellectual humility and perspective taking are effective tools to help us counteract our tendencies to cling to a limited view. Harnessing these strategies, we can expand our comprehension of multiple standpoints and, consequently, increase our effectiveness in navigating the political divide.

RECOGNIZING OUR LIMITATIONS AND VALUING OTHER PERSPECTIVES

I don't know everything. You don't know everything. In fact, no one knows everything. We're all in the same boat. However, humans are not necessarily good at estimating or evaluating the limitations of our knowledge.[1] So some of us know we don't know everything, and some of us don't know we don't know everything.

Thinking we know everything is influenced by . . . you guessed it, cognitive bias. Recall confirmation bias from Chapter 4— we pay attention to information that supports what we already believe to be true and ignore or dismiss information that conflicts with our beliefs. This shields us from thinking that we might not know everything. In fact, when you're only slightly knowledgeable about politics, you have the greatest tendency to overestimate your expertise; once you learn more, you recognize how much is beyond your grasp.[2] What could help you counteract these biases? That would be intellectual humility.

Intellectual humility consists of recognizing the limitations of our own values, beliefs, and worldview, as well as having an appreciation for others' knowledge, and it is associated with openness to learning from others.[3] In order to accurately assess our knowledge, we need to think about our own thinking, and people have varied capacities for this "metacognition." We also may be less open to new information as a response to a threat or if we view ourselves as expert in a specific field.[4] Those who are intellectually humble are seen as nicer than intellectually arrogant people, smarter than those who lack confidence, and more likeable than either of the other two.[5]

Intellectual humility is not the same as uncertainty. You can hold strong convictions and still recognize that your commitment to your beliefs tends to cause predictable biases. These biases get amplified when you surround yourself with like-minded people. You don't need to disavow your view; you need only to consider the possibility that seriously engaging other perspectives can help you hold your own view in a more balanced way. Intellectual humility helps us to be righteous without being self-righteous.

Qualities of Intellectual Humility

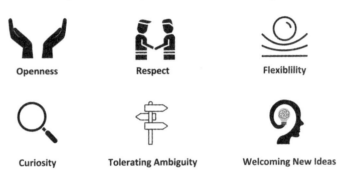

Openness   Respect   Flexiblility

Curiosity   Tolerating Ambiguity   Welcoming New Ideas

As you learned in Chapter 4, our minds are predisposed to view our perspectives as rational, unbiased, and moral and others' as irrational, biased, and self-serving. Certainly, this makes it difficult for us to impartially evaluate the accuracy of the information we believe to be true. To counteract this skewed assessment of our own knowledge, we need to de-center our beliefs.[6] Intellectual humility can help us to do so.

As a researcher, I strive to be intellectually humble. For example, there was the time I had helped with the development and facilitation of a training for police on working with LGBTQ communities. During the training, what stood out to me was pushback from some of the officers—they challenged the data we presented, weren't fully engaged, and questioned the need for training. I was interested in understanding what contributed to these dynamics, curious to see if there were particular aspects of the training that sparked their resistance. My graduate students had taken copious notes during the sessions, and we reviewed them together to identify all the instances of resistance. But then we noticed something: Resistance wasn't the only response to the training. There were also numerous instances of receptiveness to the training—officers generating ideas for supporting LGBTQ communities, participating actively in scenarios, and even countering resistance from coworkers.[7] My initial lens was focused on resistance, but with an open mind, I was able to see that opposition wasn't the whole story.

In recognizing the limitations of our current knowledge, intellectual humility renders us more motivated to learn. It might encourage us to deliberately search for information that challenges our views.[8] We're aware of sources that support our beliefs, but what have we not been exposed to? Can we find disconfirming evidence, or at least something that presents us with an alternative valid perspective?

This recognition that valid multiple perspectives exist is a strength. Instead of considering your view as *the* correct one, you might view it as *a* correct one. Take immigration, for example. One side emphasizes the terrible conditions in the home countries of refugees and the history of the United States as a country of immigrants. The other side points to the impact of large numbers of immigrants on border communities and concerns about undermining legal immigration processes. Is it possible to recognize all these points as valid? Even if you, personally, prioritize some of these concerns over others, can you acknowledge that there may be multiple reasonable ways of viewing this issue?

Rather than seeing contradictory positions as affronts to yours, can you welcome opportunities to gain insight into alternative ways of viewing things? Imagine if we saw our different perspectives as complementary rather than competing. As it happens, a single perspective is limiting, and intellectual humility is good for us: In addition to reducing dogmatism and fostering openness to learning from those with whom we disagree,[9] recognizing the limits of our knowledge is associated with emotional stability, self-confidence, and life satisfaction.[10]

PERSPECTIVE TAKING

People often say, "Explain to me how . . . " followed by something like "people can follow a leader who is corrupt," "people vote against their own interests," or "people can put their own children in danger." And then they go on to tell me why these people are extremist idiots. Did they actually want me to explain to them, or were they just looking to reinforce their view? I sometimes check: "Do you really want to understand why someone might do these things?" This gives them pause, or at least interrupts the diatribe, and for those who say yes, I lead them down a path of perspective taking.

If we judge someone else's conclusions through the lens of our own values, assumptions, and experiences, we are not perspective taking. If we try to understand from within their values, assumptions, and experiences, their conclusions make sense. That's perspective taking.

Perspective taking is a teachable skill that helps us to put ourselves in another person's shoes, thus gaining insight into their view. Perspective taking has numerous benefits, including prejudice reduction, fostering moral reasoning, and conflict resolution.[11] Furthermore, if someone feels like you strive to put yourself in their shoes and truly understand things from their perspective, they will perceive you as empathic, likable, and similar to them, and they will behave in more generous and helpful ways toward you.[12]

It's important to ground your perspective taking in accurate knowledge of others. You might gather information via direct observation and interaction,[13] as well as through writings and recordings by and about them. Although it's challenging to do so, make an effort to keep the lens you're using—whether your own observations or commentary by others—from being clouded by bias. Relying on stereotypes can lead you to erroneous conclusions that may serve to support rather than challenge your existing mental representations of others. Gathering information is one aspect of perspective taking; another is gaining insight into how others might view things.[14]

Here are some strategies you can try to gain insight into someone else's perspective:

1. Bring to mind a person whose views differ from your
   own. Rather than think about a broad category of people
   or political views, try to imagine a specific person who is
   not a public figure or spokesperson for the other side. Try
   to think of someone who is like you in some respects or
   who has had some similar life experiences.[15] To be sure,
   you are both carbon-based life-forms, but can you think
   of similarities beyond that? Do you both have children?
   Did you attend the same school? Do you have professional interests or hobbies in common? Are your podcast
   and Netflix queues aligned?

2. Notice when you are making a judgment about this other
   person. This can be a cue that there's something about
   their viewpoint you may not have considered. Try taking
   a pause in your judgment to investigate instead.[16] Take
   this opportunity to explore possible motivations for their
   opinions or behaviors. Can you generate reasons that you
   might see as positive or aligned with your values? Can
   you imagine how they would frame their own behavior?

3. It can be difficult to imagine someone else's perspective,
   especially when you've been exposed to messages about
   the ignorance, hypocrisy, and moral failings of their side.
   When you find yourself relying on these judgments as

explanations, try to stretch beyond these limited accounts for their behavior. You might see if there's a situation you've been in that's analogous to their circumstances and recall what that was like for you.[17] This could include reflecting on a time you felt you were treated unfairly or a time you felt like those in power were not supporting your rights or values.

4. You might try on one of their basic assumptions and notice how you would behave if you viewed things in a similar way. For example, "If I believed an election had been stolen, I would have taken to the streets in protest," or "If I thought the best thing for my child's mental health was to support the gender they say they are, I would advocate for availability of treatment."

5. Some additional strategies may be helpful in perspective taking.[18] For example, notice ways in which the other person is similar to yourself or to most people. You might also contrast them with the assumptions you have of people on the other side. Try considering their context—what situational factors are going on in their life? You can also reflect on your previous interactions and relationship with that person, either in your mind or by talking with a third party. These approaches can all help to consider the multidimensionality of the other person rather than flattening them into a stereotype driven by cognitive bias.

6. Since we're fighting an uphill battle against our own distorted thinking, our notions of others' views may be off base. Thus, it can be helpful to seek out perspectives from other people who hold those views[19] If you're interacting with the other person, there are some additional possibilities and challenges.[20] Really focusing your attention on the other person, noticing details and facial expressions, can help you to get a sense of them. When your emotions are activated, it can be difficult to maintain this sort of focus, so you can harness calming strategies for yourself, such as deep breathing. You can also simply ask the other person about their thoughts, feelings, and motivations. Eliciting this information may provide even greater insight if you use multiple modes of communicating—for example, text, phone, and in person.

7. As you try perspective taking, it's helpful to evaluate your success in considering another viewpoint.[21] You might test your hypotheses against viewpoints expressed by people with a similar opinion. Are they consistent with the reasons you generated for a differing set of beliefs or actions? Notice where you've gotten a clear sense of another perspective, as well as what you've missed so you can continue honing your ability to broaden your view.

In addition to engaging in perspective taking ourselves, we may find opportunities to gently encourage others to do so. This

Perspective Taking Strategies

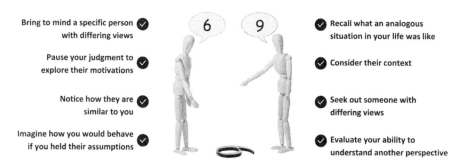

Bring to mind a specific person with differing views

Pause your judgment to explore their motivations

Notice how they are similar to you

Imagine how you would behave if you held their assumptions

Recall what an analogous situation in your life was like

Consider their context

Seek out someone with differing views

Evaluate your ability to understand another perspective

is probably most effective when practiced with people on your own side of the political spectrum. For example, I frequently hear friends on the Left frame working-class Republicans as "voting against their own interests" because they are supporting tax breaks for the rich and the dismantling of social services and unions. I sometimes challenge them to broaden their view by replying with a humorous tone, "I know, it's terrible when people vote against their economic interests, like rich Democrats, who vote for higher taxes, what a travesty." I add that, in other circumstances, we would laud those who vote for their values over their pocketbooks. They invariably pause and then admit that they hadn't really thought about it that way before. This is a tricky type of intervention as you can only challenge in this way if it's perceived as non-shaming and is coming from someone with solid credibility as being on the same side. Ideally, we work to do this in our own minds, to challenge ourselves to see things from a different view.

PRACTICING PERSPECTIVE TAKING

I remember the moment in the middle of the pandemic when I got the vaccine. I had been eligible for a while based on my age, but I hadn't gotten around to it, which seemed silly after I walked into CVS without an appointment and was vaccinated and out in fifteen minutes. Truthfully, though, it wasn't at the top of my priorities. With a seemingly endless to-do list of work, household maintenance, friends and family, and travel, it sort of slipped my mind.

It took a Facebook friend getting sick and reminding everyone to get vaccinated for me to take action to protect my health. And I'm glad I did because shingles is no joke. Oh, I'm sorry, did you think I was talking about the COVID vaccine? Oh, no—I got that as soon as I possibly could without butting in front of someone who needed it more. It's the shingles vaccine that I finally got.

Just about everyone around me had gotten the COVID vaccine as soon as it was available to them, posting photos on Facebook to celebrate and encourage others without rubbing it in the faces of those who didn't put it high on their priority list. I was in a community of pro-vaxxers. People around me were outraged by anyone who didn't wear masks and pitied those who hadn't gotten vaccinated—who had fallen prey to political rhetoric that was endangering their health and prolonging the pandemic for everyone. Those people were uncaring idiots from the vantage point of my friends and family.

Shingles is not equivalent to COVID in terms of public health consequences or political polarization, but the fact that I hadn't gotten it right away gave me pause, and I decided to use the opportunity to try a little perspective taking on what might keep people from getting the COVID vaccine. What kinds of barriers was I experiencing, and could that help me understand what stood in the way of other people getting a different type of vaccine?

One basic reason I hadn't gotten the shingles vaccine earlier was that I had a lot going on in my life, and it wasn't my top priority. I'm good about preventative health care that happens on a regular basis—every time I get my teeth cleaned, I make an appointment for my next dental cleaning six months later. But if there's something that happens infrequently, and I need to take the initiative to schedule an appointment, the referrals from my primary care physician pile up with my unopened mail and Trader Joe's receipts. Eventually, I'll schedule "make health-care appointments" into my calendar on a day without too many meetings that would interfere with my ability to answer the phone when the doctor's office calls back. Granted, it was harder to forget about the COVID vaccine, given the public health and Facebook messaging I was exposed to on a regular basis. Nonetheless, making time for health care can be a barrier.

In my efforts to be well informed about my health care, I read about the possible side effects of the shingles vaccine. I knew it might affect my energy for several days. I looked at my calendar, filled with speaking engagements, podcast interviews, and faculty commitments to identify the ideal timing for the vaccine. I scheduled the shot such that my calendar was fairly open for the two days following. It turned out I needed that—my energy was zapped, and my mind was fuzzy for a day and a half after the shot. As busy as I am, I found a way to carve out some time with few responsibilities, but that's even more of a challenge for people who have less flexibility and control over their schedules. For example, what were parents to do? If you're responsible for young children, how can you possibly find a time when no one needs you for two days? I could see how convincing people to prioritize preventative health care over the immediate needs of family was a hard sell.

I also looked into the literature to understand what kept people from getting their kids vaccinated. In addition to religious convictions, there's the belief that children need to be exposed to germs to build their immune system. If kids' environments are too pure, if they are never allowed to fall in the dirt, if they are overprotected, they will be susceptible to illness. Back in the day, when a child had chicken pox, parents would bring their kids over and rub them up against the sick child so they would get the disease and then be protected from it. I hear people on all sides of the political spectrum expressing the benefits of natural immunity, but when people on the political Right cite this as a reason not to get their kids vaccinated against COVID, they get bashed by the political Left.

Furthermore, parents express concerns about risks associated with vaccines.[22] In fact, people tend to perceive consequences that arise from their actions as riskier than those that are consequences of inaction.[23] So if your kid has a reaction to a vaccine, you feel worse than if they get sick because they're not vaccinated. If the vaccine cost-benefit analysis is not an absolute, and rather a matter of where you draw the line, it's easier to see how parents make the choices they do.

It turns out, the key determinants of parental vaccine hesitancy are trusting relationships with health-care providers, sources of information, social norms, and general beliefs about health.[24] In the context of COVID, an additional layer of beliefs impacted vaccine uptake. On top of concerns about safety and efficacy, the decision not to get vaccinated as an expression of personal liberty was an added factor.[25] Bodily autonomy is important to people across the political spectrum. People on the Right may apply it more readily to vaccines, whereas people on the Left are apt to support autonomy in reproductive choice. In either case, the argument against autonomy is grounded in protecting those who are vulnerable, which is accompanied by self-righteous accusations that the other side is selfish.

Even later, when we got to the second and third round of boosters, I started hearing my friends on the Left making more nuanced choices about vaccines. Some had strong physical reactions to the first dose and so were weighing the pros and cons of getting another. Some wanted to hold back and see how it was working for others before they jumped on the bandwagon. This sounded a lot like the vaccine hesitancy on the Right, yet I never heard anyone acknowledge that they were coming around to seeing things from the opposition's perspective.

I hear people on the Left saying vaccines and masking were politicized by people on the Right. Yet, those on the Left also fell into politicization, labeling everyone who hadn't gotten the vaccine immediately as "anti-vaxxers." A year into the pandemic, when public health officials first told us we could remove our masks (this was pre-Delta variant), a friend confided that he was hesitant to do so, not because he felt he was at risk, but because he was worried that, unmasked, he would be mistaken for a Republican. This behavior was not based in science but rather in tribalism and performative politics.

As I write this, three years into the pandemic, messaging about COVID vaccines has shifted considerably. We accept that the shot will not necessarily keep us from getting infected, but that it will reduce the risk of serious illness and death. There is a more nuanced framing of the efficacy than was touted initially. When a newly available medication is fast-tracked through FDA approval, and when mandatory uptake is being considered, it's no wonder some people resist.

As you read this, you may object to the false equivalence. Perhaps you're noting the difference between getting a booster and getting the initial COVID shot or between chicken pox and a global pandemic. You might argue that bodily autonomy is not the same in the case of vaccines and abortion. There's no question that there are differences. But there are also similarities. Perspective taking relies on harnessing the similarities to try to develop genuine understanding of another person's situation and view. If you look only at the differences, you are missing the opportunity to comprehend your fellow humans. The insight you gain may quell your outrage, boost your intellectual humility, and make you a more effective advocate.

After going through this exercise, I shared this on Facebook: "Reflecting on why people haven't gotten the COVID vaccine made me think of all the health care that I haven't gotten around to. For example, I've been eligible for the shingles vaccine for 5 years, and it took a Facebook friend posting about getting shingles to get me to CVS for a shot. Is there anything you need to do for your health? Are you due for a colonoscopy? mammogram? prostate exam? pap smear? eye exam? If so, please consider this a gentle remind to take care of your health. Also, if you want to try a perspective taking activity, reflect on what's kept you from preventative health care and consider if some of these reasons also help to explain why people haven't gotten the COVID vaccine yet (*spoiler alert* it's not all about politics and misinformation, even if some of it is)."[26]

Perspective taking is not about changing your mind; it's about broadening it. A single view limits us; the ability to hold multiple perspectives is a strength. Understanding others is key to surviving the pandemic and for our democracy to survive political polarization.

MEANING MAKING

Cognitive biases not only influence the characteristics we associate with other people; they also affect the meaning we make of their views. In the height of COVID, I heard a lot of this: "I think everyone should get vaccinated because that will reduce the overall impact of the pandemic, so if you don't get vaccinated you're selfish," as well as this: "I am against vaccine mandates because I trust people to make their own medical decisions, so if you are for vaccine mandates, you want to take away people's rights." What both sides were doing here was framing the other side's motivations as the opposite of their own. They were flipping the meaning the issue had for them and attributing the converse to the other side. This is typically a poor representation of the other side's actual motivations. Rather, it creates a willful misunderstanding of the meaning something has for someone else based on the meaning it has for you.

As each side portrays the other, I see a lot of flipped meanings. For example, someone who opposes abortion because they want to protect the lives of children will posit that pro-choice people must not care about children. On the other hand, a person who advocates for access to abortion because they want to protect women's autonomy will frame pro-life people as tolerant of women's enslavement. I also hear people pointing out the logical fallacies of the other side. Pro-choice advocates point to pro-life people who support the death penalty and oppose gun control, whereas pro-life advocates note the lack of choice for an unborn child or for a woman who feels unsupported in carrying a pregnancy to term.

Such rhetorical strategies that emphasize our opponents' illogic and immorality reinforce our certainty that we are justified in our views. However, our feelings of righteousness are resting on the shaky ground of contrasting ourselves with one-dimensional stereotypes of the other side. The inaccuracy of the allegations resonate only with those who are already firmly situated on one side or the other, limiting the potential to engage those who are less committed, let alone people who have views that are vastly different from our own. Our assessment of other people's motivations is related to motive attribution asymmetry—our tendency to frame our side as benevolent and the other side as malicious. Notice when you're viewing things through this lens, and see if you've simply flipped your meaning and attributed it to the other side. When we disagree, it doesn't mean I value the opposite of what you hold so dear. More likely, it means I attribute a different meaning than you do.

Furthermore, our willful misunderstanding of others renders us ineffective strategists. What if we try to comprehend how things make sense to people who disagree with us rather than double down on our limited view of how these things make sense to us? Wherever you stand, try lifting up your values without putting down people whose views are different from yours. Let's humanize rather than demonize those who disagree with us. Not only will this help you cultivate compassion, but understanding what might draw people to an opposing camp will also enable you to state your case from their frame of reference, making you a more effective advocate.

BARRIERS TO BROADENING OUR MINDS

When I lay out the evidence to support intellectual humility, some people recognize the benefits yet hesitate to relinquish their mental constraints. Are you feeling resistant to the prospect of broadening your mind? Let's unpack some possible reasons for this resistance.

What if your narrow, singular perspective is right? What if the people on the other side really are selfish, hateful idiots or are inexplicably supporting a position you think is harmful to individuals or society as a whole? What if, by finding ways to see things from a different view, you fall prey to their malevolent schemes? It's possible that these types of questions are rooted in fear of naivete and the possible consequences of being a Pollyanna. We may attempt to avoid gullibility, feeling it's smarter to be on our guard. The important thing to keep in mind is that seeing multiple possible perspectives doesn't eliminate the possibility that our original hypothesis was correct. It allows us to hold our existing belief as an option while testing alternative theories. This approach promotes mental flexibility and is aligned with the scientific method.

Perhaps you are concerned that intellectual humility is anathema to critical thinking. It's true that critical thinking is a valuable skill, and it will be enhanced as we embrace a view that helps us gain new insight. Keep in mind that humans are predisposed to double down on what we already believe to be true, so it's not difficult for us to dig our heels into our existing beliefs. When we apply our minds to take in information at our disposal, analyze it, and articulate our conclusions, we strengthen one aspect of critical thinking, but we ignore another. We can render our minds stronger and more nimble when we challenge our biases and stretch to grasp a perspective we don't already hold.

Perhaps you are nervous that intellectual humility will weaken your convictions and reduce your motivation to act. This might be a barrier if you have an activist orientation, but otherwise, it may not make such a difference. Perhaps you're more contemplative and less activist. If this is your natural inclination, embracing intellectual humility may fit well and not threaten your typical approach to politics.[27] It might be helpful to develop a realistic sense of the potential impact of intellectual humility by assessing your baseline propensity to engage in activism. For example, have you engaged in collective advocacy in the past, and how likely are you to participate in low-risk (e.g., sign a petition) and high-risk activism (e.g., get arrested)?[28] It may be that your level of activism would not be much affected by your degree of singular conviction.

Although you don't need to renounce your deeply held values to embrace intellectual humility, you may become aware of your arguments' limitations or you may notice ways in which they are subject to the same critiques you've made of your opponents' views. Keep in mind that broadening your mind does not mean your previously held view was wrong. It simply means there is another perspective that is potentially valid.

It can be challenging to lay down our swords, remove our armor, and stand in the naked vulnerability of not knowing. Unquestioned certitude may offer a sense of security and well-being, whereas opening our beliefs up to inquiry can disrupt our equilibrium and may threaten our sense of self in connection with others.[29] Given the psychological consequences of uncertainty, what makes it worth the effort to broaden our minds? Broadening our views can yield a more comprehensive understanding of the political and human landscape, which will help us make sense of the world and empower us to strengthen our advocacy skills, our interpersonal relationships, and our democracy.

KEY TAKEAWAYS

- Grasping only a small slice of reality is disempowering; the ability to understand multiple perspectives can help you achieve your goals.

- Intellectual humility can help you recognize the limits of your own knowledge without forcing you to change your position on an issue.

- Perspective taking is a good strategy to gain insight into other people's views.

- Different views don't necessarily indicate opposite morality; sometimes they arise from varied meanings.

- You may feel some hesitation to broaden your mind, but intellectual humility and perspective taking will benefit you in the long run.

CHAPTER 7

Open Your Heart

On October 7, 2023, Hamas attacks Israel. Hundreds of civilians are killed or abducted, young people at a music festival slaughtered, women raped, bodies mutilated, people barricaded in their homes crying for help. The next day, there are public celebrations of the attacks, people gathering to cheer the violence as liberatory. Where is the compassion?

Two months of Israel's retaliatory strikes later, the body count hits 20,000 in Gaza, mostly women and children. Nearly 1.9 million people are forced to flee their homes, displacing 85 percent of Gaza's population. Humanitarian aid struggles to reach malnourished children as food, water, and medicine run out. Scarcity of fuel and shelter drive families to shiver in tents. And yet, the bombing continues. Where is the compassion?

Viewed through these lenses, compassion appears to be in short supply. Considered in another way, caring is abundant. Israelis, Jews, and many others around the world mourn the losses of October 7, and pray for safe return of the hostages. Meanwhile, the crisis in Gaza engenders worldwide attention to the plight of Palestinians and tremendous sympathy for those suffering through the mass death and destruction. There is considerable openhearted concern for both sides of the conflict. Nonetheless, not everyone offers warmth evenly—some feel empathy in an imbalanced way—less for one side than the other.

As I was working on this book in the fall of 2023, I became fascinated by a study about this lopsided empathy. In the study "How Empathic Concern Fuels Political Polarization,"[1] researchers identified people high in empathic concern—those who have a "tendency to experience other-oriented emotions, such as sympathy or compassion, for another person who is in distress." Participants read a scenario in which a campus talk was shut down by a politically affiliated protester who struck an audience member. Participants who were both generally empathic and identified strongly with their political party were keen to shut down a speaker from the other party. They also had less concern for the injured bystander. This wasn't the case for those who were generally *less* empathic or who didn't have a strong connection to a political party.

The authors concluded that the combination of partisanship and empathy drives people to care deeply about their in-group and be particularly attuned to injuries committed by opponents. As a result, compared to less empathic people, partisan empaths are more prone to support censorship of the outgroup and demonstrate less sympathy for their suffering. Ironically, the more empathic we are, the more animosity we may feel toward those across the political divide.

This study helped me make sense of people's reactions to the Israel-Hamas war. I was hearing from tenderhearted people on both sides who seemed fairly unconcerned about the suffering of those in the other camp. They were concentrating their empathy solely on the side they affiliated with and honing in on the harm done by, and not done to, those on the other side. Thus, in a politically polarized situation, tapping into empathy is not enough. We must generate empathy for people on the other side in order to avert further demonizing people across the political spectrum.

EMPATHY AND COMPASSION

A resident of South Florida gets a knock at their door. It's a volunteer from an LGBTQ organization who is talking to voters about a referendum to repeal rights of transgender people. The canvasser defines the term "transgender," asks the resident their opinion on the law, and then shows them a video with arguments on both sides of the issue. Prompted by the canvasser, the resident describes a time they felt negative judgment or stigma directed toward them for being different, and the canvasser encourages them to think about how their own experience might help them understand what it's like to be transgender. The canvasser then asks if the conversation changed the resident's views about transgender people or the referendum, thanks the resident, and leaves.

Hundreds of voters took part in these ten-minute conversations as part of an experiment.[2] Participants who took the perspective of transgender people reported more positive attitudes and greater support for laws protecting transgender rights than those who talked with canvassers about other issues. Furthermore, the effects were lasting and quite substantial, the equivalent of changes in Americans' attitudes toward lesbians and gay men over a fourteen-year period.

Although empathy is a natural quality that spontaneously arises when people are faced with someone in distress,[3] we can further cultivate this concern for others through intention and practice. Perspective taking, which we learned about in Chapter 6, is a cognitive activity that can reduce animosity and generate support for people who are different from oneself. This mental shift can arouse empathic understanding, getting inside someone's emotional experience, not simply their life circumstances. So, if you want to extend empathy toward people across the political spectrum, try seeing things from their perspective.

How might you go about generating empathy via perspective taking? One approach is to imagine what it would be like for you to be in a particular situation. For example, if you're having trouble understanding why workers join unions, you could consider what you would do if you saw people around you injured on the job, and the union was advocating for safer working conditions. Another approach is to imagine what it's like for a person who is in that situation—in trying to understand the management side of labor negotiations, you could try to take the perspective of the owner of a business considering potential layoffs due to higher wages. Both strategies work, but be aware that imagining yourself in the situation can also provoke distress.[4] Whereas empathy is an emotional experience of another person's feelings, compassion goes a step further, to not only feel their distress, but to genuinely desire to alleviate their suffering as well.[5] Compassion can improve our health and even help us live longer—volunteers who are motivated to benefit others have decreased mortality risk compared to those who do so for self-serving reasons.[6]

Although compassion is a natural human quality with evolutionary advantages, in the face of threats or scarce resources, more self-centered motives may prevail.[7] Furthermore, compassion may be framed differently by people across the political spectrum, with liberals offering direct assistance and conservatives helping people to help themselves.[8] The ensuing policy battles further entrench division. In this way, political polarization can clog our natural wellspring of caring.

EQUANIMITY

Simply being an empathic person does not necessarily reduce polarization. As you learned earlier in the chapter, people who score high on empathy tend to direct it toward people on their own side and maximize animosity toward their adversaries.

Apparently, the question is not how to be more openhearted generally, but rather how to cultivate compassion toward people on the other side. This might be easier if we view them as less "on the other side" than our cognitive biases would have us believe. What we are striving for here is an aspect of what Buddhists call "equanimity" or "having an equal attitude towards all beings, without the boundaries that we habitually draw between friends, strangers, and those we consider 'difficult people.'"[9]

To cultivate equanimity, we can look for similarities between ourselves and other people. Along these lines, Buddhist nun Pema Chödrön describes her simple practice of "Just Like Me" in her 2019 book, *Welcoming the Unwelcome: Wholehearted Living in a Brokenhearted World.* You can try this by focusing your attention on a person in a public place—a park, a traffic jam, a supermarket checkout line—and thinking to yourself, "Just like me, this person wants to feel safe and comfortable. Just like me, this person gets frustrated. Just like me, this person doesn't want to be dismissed," and similar notions.

Empathy and compassion are powerful tools for healing the political divide, but only if paired with equanimity. Without equanimity, we may direct our natural sense of caring only toward those we view as our allies while we foment negativity toward those we view as the opposition. Not only does this have negative societal consequences, but it also stimulates our self-righteous aggression.

COURAGE

You may find yourself resisting the idea of being compassionate toward those on the other side of the political divide. It's scary to go against your tribe, frightening to think about your friends criticizing you, anxiety-provoking to engage with people who think differently than you do.

The root of the word "courage" is "heart." Noting this etymology, Lama Karma Yeshe Chödrön frames courage as holding our tenderness, vulnerability, and fear, even as we move forward with strength.[10] Opening your heart is a brave act.

Whereas empathy is a natural human quality, it does not arise spontaneously in the face of political polarization. People tell me that when they're having a hard time feeling openhearted toward folks across the political divide, it keeps them from reaching out to connect, makes them hesitant to repair a meaningful relationship.

In Part I of this book, we learned that the ideas you have about people on the other side of the political spectrum are distorted by the news, social media, and your own mind. In Chapter 5, we developed the inner strength to withstand challenging situations. In Chapter 6, we recognized the limitations of holding a narrow view. In this chapter, we started to cultivate compassion. With this groundwork, we are ready for courageous heart opening.

In addition to holding the intention to be openhearted, something that will support this courageous act is practice, creating a new habit to overcome ones that are not serving us as we would like. Research supports compassion training as an effective way to increase feelings of connection, even in a brief intervention,[11] and improve positive emotions, psychological health, and life satisfaction when practiced for two months.[12] Some styles of mindfulness meditation, which don't focus specifically on compassion but rather serve to calm and focus the mind, appear to be beneficial for reducing political conflict. In one study, members of the UK Parliament who underwent mindfulness training treated each other in more humane and constructive ways.[13]

There was a point in my life when I wanted to learn to meditate, so I bought a set of cassette tapes (which is some indication of how long ago I started my practice). One of the tapes was Sharon Salzberg teaching lovingkindness meditation. I listened to this tape repeatedly, flipping the cassette over and back, envisioning sending warm energy and positive wishes toward myself and others. When I moved to Santa Barbara and was seeking support for my budding inclination toward Buddhism, I found a center that gathered every Sunday morning to practice together. It so happened that the foundational practice of this center focused on compassion—envisioning beings and sending them openhearted energy. For years, it was my Sunday morning routine to attend this practice.

The point is not that everyone needs to be a Buddhist. There are many spiritual and secular traditions that encourage compassion, but how do we shift it from an aspiration to a reality? In my experience, and consistent with psychological research, forming a habit will help. Bringing forth goodwill toward others repeatedly when we are not in a stressful situation will make it easier to access when we are experiencing conflict or distress.

GUIDED VISUALIZATION

You may find yourself having a hard time generating warmth toward "those people." If so, I want to offer you a resource, a guided visualization to help cultivate compassion in the face of political division. Although it's possible to feel empathy toward an abstract category of people,[14] this activity focuses on specific individuals to promote a more powerful emotional experience.

The practice moves from focus on self to someone who is close to a neutral person to someone who is challenging. It's not uncommon for it to be harder to generate compassion toward someone who is challenging,[15] so if you find yourself reacting, I encourage you to continue the practice. I found it gets easier over time.

I adapted this guided visualization from the Buddhist loving-kindness meditation that I learned from Sharon Salzberg's recorded teachings, but you don't need to hold any particular belief to practice it. I find it to be a useful resource for keeping my heart open to people whose views and values contrast with my own. I hope you will find it beneficial as well. You can find the audio on my website at https://taniaisrael.com/cultivating-compassion/.

As I guide you through this visualization, I'll be asking you to direct goodwill toward yourself and others in the form of these thoughts: "May you be free from harm. May you be healthy and happy. May you grow with ease."

1. Sit in a comfortable position, close your eyes or lower your gaze, and take a few slow, deep breaths.

2. Now, think to yourself, "May I be free from harm. May I be healthy and happy. May I grow with ease." Repeat these phrases to yourself slowly, reflecting on each one as you send yourself these warm-hearted messages.

3. Next, conjure in your mind a person who is close to you and who you don't have any difficulty feeling goodwill toward. Think of someone who looks at politics the same way you do; you feel comfortable in their presence, knowing how they view things. Direct these thoughts toward this person: "May you be free from harm. May you be healthy and happy. May you grow with ease." Mentally repeat these phrases as you keep this close person in mind.

4. Now, imagine a neutral person—someone whose politics you don't know, or perhaps politics isn't central to your connection. It might be the checkout clerk at the super-market, a coworker, or someone you pass regularly as you walk in the park. Hold them in your mind as you repeat a few times: "May you be free from harm. May you be healthy and happy. May you grow with ease."

5. Finally, think of a challenging person—someone who votes or has values different from your own, whose views poke at you, perhaps someone with whom you've had conflict about politics. Identify a specific person rather than a group of people. Send them these hopes: "May you be free from harm. May you be healthy and happy.

May you grow with ease." Repeat these phrases in your mind several times as you picture this person.

6. Allow the visualization to dissolve as you take a few more breaths, resting in a sense of connection to yourself and others.

7. When you feel ready, open your eyes.

This visualization is something I draw on to keep my heart open. You may have other tools grounded in your faith or from other sources. I find it helpful to prepare myself by doing this repeatedly when I'm not in the midst of a challenging interaction. I approach it as a practice, something I do over and over to reinforce habits that bring me into alignment.

KEY TAKEAWAYS

- Perspective taking can stimulate an emotional response that reduces animosity toward people who are different from oneself.

- Empathy (experiencing another person's emotions) and compassion (the desire to alleviate another's suffering) are natural human qualities.

- Equanimity is important to counteract the tendency to direct empathy only toward one's own side.

- Compassion can be cultivated through practice.

PART III

Strengthening Connection

Spoiler alert for *The Wizard of Oz In *The Wizard of Oz*, Dorothy starts down the Yellow Brick Road all by herself and then meets her companions along the way. The Scarecrow, Tin Man, and Cowardly Lion are each on a quest for something: The Scarecrow wants a brain; the Tin Man, a heart; and the Cowardly Lion seeks courage. They hope the all-powerful wizard can bestow these qualities on them, but in truth, he is simply a man, who can only reflect back what each did not see in themselves. And it turns out, that's all they really need.

What does this children's story have to do with political polarization? We may be perceiving our leaders as the wizards who have the only power to solve things. We may want the politicians to stop fighting, the social media companies to make their platforms less divisive, and the influencers to tone down their hostile rhetoric. But, truly, the power to reduce polarization is already within each of us.

In Part II of this book, you tended to your internal resources. You fostered intellectual humility and compassion, and you learned to face challenges. You have the brain, heart, and courage to navigate political polarization. Plus, you know something Dorothy and her friends never gleaned—the other side is not what they seemed to be.

My mother recalled seeing *The Wizard of Oz* in the theater as a young child. She recounted to me how terrifying she found the Wicked Witch of the West and the flying monkeys. Later, when she watched it with me on TV, the villains were not so scary; they were smaller on the TV than on the movie screen, and she had the benefit of maturity.

Part I of this book might have helped you rightsize your fear of political adversaries. Perhaps they don't feel as scary now that you know they are not as extreme and belligerent as you once believed. Part II may have further shifted your associations with people across the political spectrum, akin to what my mother experienced when I took her to see the musical *Wicked* for her seventieth birthday.

Spoiler alert for *Wicked* When we see the Oz story through the eyes of the Wicked Witch of the West, she's not so wicked, after all. She has a name, Elphaba. She has a history. She has feelings and longing and dreams. There are reasons for her actions that Dorothy and her companions cannot fathom. And she and the good witch, who start out as enemies, end up dear friends, who help each other grow. Seeing this, my mother was no longer scared of the witch. Furthermore, she understood and felt compassion for her.

So, now having journeyed through Parts I and II of this book, we have a more accurate view of people across the political spectrum, and we're calm, curious, and compassionate. We're doing great! Why complicate matters by interacting with other people? What do we have to gain by stretching beyond ourselves?

To be sure, whether or not you choose to engage with others is up to you. It's an opportunity, not a mandate. You're welcome to set this book down right now and go about your business. Perhaps you met your goals for reducing stress about political conflict. If so, I am delighted that you got something out of this book, and I wish you well.

But what if, equipped with a more accurate view of others and robust body, mind, and heart, you feel prepared, and perhaps even excited, to do more? Having turned down the volume of polarizing input and applying the skills you learned in Part II, you're now in an excellent position to engage beyond yourself. Indeed, you have cultivated yourself as fertile ground for healthy connections with others to take root.

Strengthening connection requires a closeness that polarization makes difficult. Ideally, learning to withstand challenging situations (Chapter 5), recognizing the limitations of our narrow thinking (Chapter 6), and building emotional bridges across differences (Chapter 7) have created a foundation to ease the bumpiness of engaging beyond ourselves.

Not only will interpersonal engagement help us navigate political polarization; it will benefit our well-being as well. Social connectedness is a basic human need that can lower stress and even reduce the risk of premature death, suggesting that "connection culture" rather than "cancel culture" will benefit us individually and as a society.[1]

Despite what we witness in the media, many Americans are eager to connect, even across political lines. Most Democrats and Republicans have had constructive conversations across political differences, and a growing percentage of adults in the United States say they work together to solve problems in their community with people who have a different political view.[2] Even in the face of increased societal conflict, we are forging bonds and collaborating.

Part III will offer a road map to strengthening connections in a divided nation. Chapter 8 will help you engage with people across the political divide, Chapter 9 describes a multitude of avenues to participate in community and country, and Chapter 10 exhibits the bridging movement—even if you don't choose to join, learning about it will make you more optimistic about Americans and the future of our country.

In *The Wizard of Oz*, Dorothy wants to go home, to return to Kansas. Only she can't return home without realizing something about herself and others. Like her companions, she had what she needed within herself all along. You may want to return home, to a more familiar way of viewing yourself and your political adversaries. You may balk at the effort it takes to be empathic, to try to understand a view that is not your own, to keep your heart open. Strengthening connections will support you on this final leg of the journey home.

Dorothy and her companions needed each other. Each alone was vulnerable and afraid. The Yellow Brick Road crew protected and encouraged each other. They were able to accomplish their goals through interdependence and connection. Joined with Americans along the full spectrum of political views, you will be healthier, stronger, and more effective than you could possibly be on your own. So, let's link arms and complete our journey together!

CHAPTER 8

Engage Effectively across the Divide

After writing a book about how to have dialogue across political lines, I heard about tremendous successes in bridging the divide. People reported that they reached out to their family members, coworkers, neighbors, and manicurists. There was a woman who left my book in the bathroom for her husband to read as a step toward reconnection. Particularly touching was when my friend Nancy's stepbrother was dying. It was the middle of the pandemic, and he needed help. She wanted to go care for him, but as a bisexual feminist lawyer, she wasn't sure how she would be able to tolerate his Trumpian, Fox News–watching lifestyle. She told me, "Tania, I'm packing your book to get me through this," and she stayed by his side through the end of his life. Later, she shared with me how she was able to have meaningful conversations with her stepbrother about their differing views.

People have strong motivations for bridging divides—they want to stay connected with someone they care about, they want to persuade or convince someone to see things as they do, they want to find common ground or heal the divide, or they want to gain insight into a perspective that seems unfathomable to them. Yet they have competing motivations as well. They also want to have their opinions validated, they want to have their views mirrored back to them, they want to be seen. They want to express their views freely and immediately, in an unconstrained manner. They worry that, if they don't contradict something they see as wrongheaded, they will be bad allies, they will reinforce the other person's wrong views, or, worst of all, the other person will think they agree with them!

One of the most important lessons I've learned in doing this work on dialogue is that people have more than one want. You will be at your best if you're aware of these multiple desires and make decisions about whether and how to engage across political differences, keeping in mind what draws you to dialogue and what can trip you up.

Have you tried to engage in dialogue with someone whose political views differ from yours? If so, how did it go? I asked folks on Twitter and LinkedIn, and here's what they said: "yes, and it was helpful" (72 percent), "yes, and it didn't go well" (17 percent), "no, but I'm open to it" (11 percent), and "no, and I'm not interested" (0 percent).[1] It's encouraging that most people had a positive experience, and it's not surprising that it didn't go well sometimes. When I ask people what's working for them and what's particularly challenging, these are some of the key insights: (1) Listening is a powerful tool. (2) It's important to have reasonable expectations for the outcome of dialogue. (3) It's good to have an exit strategy when it's time to wrap up or when the conversation isn't productive. Let's look at how to put dialogue strategies into practice so you can have more satisfying interactions with people who disagree with you politically.

Have you tried to engage in dialogue with someone whose political views differ from yours? If so, how did it go?

Yes, and it was helpful	72%
Yes, and it didn't go well.	17%
No, but I'm open to it	11%
No, and I'm not interested	0%

Souce: Aggregated data from LinkedIn and Twitter Poll

SETTING THE STAGE

Curiosity is the best attitude for going into conversations across differences. As the other person senses your genuine desire to understand rather than confront them, they will be less defensive and more likely to open up to you. It's important that you feel and convey authentic interest rather than simply asserting that you're curious. Saying, "I'm curious about how you can hold that position," and then enumerating evidence to the contrary communicates that you want to make your point more than you want to hear from them.

Some people dismiss curiosity, worrying that focusing attention on an opposing perspective will betray their own beliefs. Keep in mind what you learned about intellectual humility in Chapter 6—you don't need to compromise your values to be interested in and respectful of someone else's perspective.

Remember that just because someone has a different viewpoint doesn't mean they are the caricature of the most bombastic extremist you're familiar with from the media. Cognitive biases are likely driving your assumptions that they are uninformed and unkind. That said, you may have some less-than-knowledgeable conflict junkies in your life who confirm the worst stereotypes. You get to make choices about whom you have these conversations with. So maybe don't start with your ranting uncle, and instead approach the cousin who always gets up to clear the table when the fireworks start.

People often ask me what to do when they have a history of political arguments with someone, but they want to try again. If you've had challenging interactions in the past, it's helpful to communicate your intention to do things differently. You might say something like, "I know we've had difficulty talking about this topic in the past, but I would like to have a different kind of conversation, one where I really try to understand where you're coming from."

You can also put the other person in a positive mindset by evoking meaningful connections, not only with you, but with others, too. When people think about their most important relationships, they are less defensive when later confronted with opposing views.[2] Thus, you might inquire about their children or other family members before you get into topics of potential disagreement. It can also be helpful to warm up by discussing some things you have in common or both care about, like your community, sports, or knitting. Accentuating similarities can lay the foundation for an easier conversation.

We prefer engaging with people who are receptive to our ideas, and the more we communicate our willingness to engage respectfully with another person's ideas, the more they will do the same. How do you convey this receptiveness? Try to explicitly express that you understand, and acknowledge points of agreement. When you do state your views, soften claims by hedging with terms like "somewhat" or "might." It can even be helpful to frame your sentences to make use of positive words rather than negative ones ("can" rather than "can't"). These tips have proven power to promote receptiveness.[3]

ENCOURAGE ELABORATION

Do you ever find yourself stumped for what to do when a person says something you disagree with? Perhaps they've referenced a study you're not familiar with. Maybe you worry it will prompt conflict if you contradict them. You might know where you stand, but you haven't developed a clearly articulated argument for it. In these situations, the easiest and most effective response is to encourage them to elaborate on what they've said. There are some tools that will come in handy.

Listening

Listening is a key tool for successful conversations across differences and an important aspect of encouraging elaboration. It is a mechanism for gathering information that will enhance your understanding of a different perspective. Listening will strengthen your connection and will even help you to persuade or find common ground. For listening to move you toward your goals, it's important to implement this skill effectively. I'll review some key listening tips here. If you want greater depth or examples, there's an entire chapter on listening in my book *Beyond Your Bubble: How to Connect Across the Political Divide, Skills and Strategies for Conversations That Work*.

I'm going to let you in on a secret about listening that it took me twenty years as a psychologist to discover. When you rearrange the letters of the word "listen," it spells "silent." When you're listening to another person, you need to allow them uninterrupted time to speak. This isn't as easy as it sounds. We often want to jump in with our own ideas or fill even the smallest gap by speaking. Instead, try nodding occasionally and uttering, "Mm-hmm," every so often. This communicates that you are listening and invites the speaker to continue.

Reflecting

Reflecting is a powerful tool. When someone speaks, rather than sharing back what you think, share back a summary of what they said. Listening in this way will help you understand them, and it will help them to feel like you care and that you understand them. Sharing one's perspective and having it reflected back can improve empathy, trust, and warmth toward the listener's group, especially when the speaker feels disenfranchised.[4] People want to be seen. If we can do this for them, we understand them, as well as generate a bond that engenders trust and forgiveness.[5]

A note about reflecting—not only do people want to know you understand them; they may also crave a mirror for their emotional state. If they are fearful, outraged, or devastated, it may feel unsatisfying to be met with a neutral statement of the content they've expressed. People are sometimes looking to bond through shared reactions. Even if you are not feeling the same way, try to demonstrate empathy for their emotional experience. I notice people appreciate even a facial expression that echoes their shock, sadness, relief, or other feelings.

Questions

People often think questions are the best way to show interest, but actually, questions often take things in the direction of the listener's interest rather than focusing on what's important to the speaker. Furthermore, peppering someone with question after question can feel like an interrogation. It's important to respond to what they're saying by reflecting and giving space before you take things in a new direction with a question. Thus, we should use questions sparingly.

When you do ask questions, keep in mind that questions can be used in combative ways, so make sure your questions are based in genuine curiosity, and don't use "gotcha" questions to box someone into a corner. Questions that ask "why" sometimes make people feel like they need to justify themselves, so try to stay away from those as well. You can rephrase a question like "Why do you support the labor union's strike?" to "How did you come to support the labor union's strike?" It's most helpful to ask questions that are open-ended (can't be answered with simply a yes or no) and that help you to understand why the speaker feels or thinks as they do.

Rather than think about your listening role in terms of asking questions, think of what you're doing as encouraging elaboration. Providing uninterrupted time to speak encourages elaboration. Reflecting encourages elaboration. Asking someone to elaborate can make them more receptive to further engagement and can make you more receptive to their view.[6] You can use phrases like these to encourage elaboration:

1. Go on. I'd like to hear more.

2. I'm curious about . . .

3. Can you tell me more about how you've come to think that?

4. Can you help me understand . . .

5. I'm interested to hear more about how that would work.

Managing Reactions

What should you do if something you hear rubs you the wrong way? Maybe it's information that conflicts with what you've been exposed to, or perhaps it's an experience that's very different from your own, or a way of framing something that's not how you've always seen it. Interacting with people who have different identities, life experiences, and values can push our buttons. We might feel vulnerable, attacked, even angry. In her book, *You're Not Listening*, Kate Murphy explains why we're not built to listen to opposing views: "The primitive brain interprets a difference of opinion as being abandoned by the tribe, alone and unprotected, so outrage and fear take over," and the part of the brain that's activated interferes with areas of the brain involved in listening.[7]

When strong emotions surface, you may respond to a sense of threat and kick into "fight, flight, or freeze" mode. If you find your heart racing and muscles tensing, try taking a few slow, deep breaths to regain your equilibrium. Even as you keep your motivations in mind, you can feel reactive, which can get in the way of connection. Try to sit with the discomfort, and see if there's something in what you're hearing that will offer more complexity to your way of thinking. For more detail on this topic, you can review Chapter 5 of this book or read the chapter on managing emotions in *Beyond Your Bubble*.

Benefits of Encouraging Elaboration

Encouraging elaboration has many benefits. It will help you understand where the other person is coming from, which is essential if you want to find common ground, persuade, or gain insight. It will also help them feel understood, which fulfills a very human need to be seen and can increase their feeling of warmth toward you. Building trust in this way can render them more open to knowledge or perspectives that you share.

Although curiosity is the best motivation for entering into dialogue across differences, there can be additional benefits beyond understanding where the other person is coming from. In fact, listening is more effective in shifting someone's views than providing facts and arguments. When people feel understood and are not challenged, their anxiety and defensiveness drops, which helps them hold more complex and less extreme views without shifting their overall position.[8]

THE FACT IS, WE SHOULD SET ASIDE FACTS

I'm often asked, "How can we have a conversation when we don't even agree on facts?" It's true, people on the political Left and Right tend to pay attention to and trust different news sources, which can lead to conflicting knowledge about an issue. In this sort of situation, you might find yourself referencing research and news articles and trying to correct misinformation. You may feel exasperated when the other person points to their data and analyses from sources you see as untrustworthy and biased.

Dialogue, Not Debate

We often picture a debate when imagining a conversation across political disagreement. We compile facts and well-reasoned arguments. We rehearse our talking points as we mentally respond to news, social media, or imagined opponents. We compare notes with our teammates, building our case and boosting our confidence. We are sure that we can articulate convincing rhetoric to appeal to the audience.

In a debate, however, the opposing team is not our intended audience. No matter how awesome we think we are, we do not expect that the other team members will hear our airtight rationale, realize the error of their thinking, and cross the stage to stand with us at our podium. Instead, when we debate, we are trying to convince outside observers—judges, spectators, voters—that we have done the best job and should be declared the winner.

There are no outside observers in dialogue. There are only two humans in conversation with one another, motivated to maintain a relationship, persuade, heal the divide, or understand. None of these goals will best be accomplished by presenting facts and arguments, no matter how accurate or compelling.

Function, Not Facts

We may feel a strong urge to provide information and a clear line of reasoning to counter the speaker's view; however, this approach is more apt to make them defensive and even dig into their position more strongly. What if we focus on the function the information serves for the person rather than the content of the facts?

I typically encourage people to shift away from competing facts and to focus instead on how the other person formed their views, the meaning that the information has for them, and how it guides their actions. These lines of inquiry focus on the function of the information and can unlock a respectful and productive exchange. This is not to say that facts don't matter; it is simply that exchanging factual information will not help people achieve their goals for dialogue.

Recall that what people hope to achieve by talking with someone across the political divide is to maintain or repair a relationship, persuade or convince, find common ground, or gain some insight into other people. Sharing facts that contrast with what someone believes to be true will not help to accomplish any of these goals; in fact, it is more likely to push someone away than to change their minds or foster closeness.

I was curious to know what other people said they want to hear from others, so I polled my LinkedIn contacts, asking, "What do you most want to know about someone else's perspective?" Only 10 percent of people were interested in knowing the source for their stats, with three times that curious to find out each of the following: how they came to their view, the meaning it has for them, and how it guides their actions.[9]

What do you most want to know about someone else's perspective?

The meaning it has for them	33%
How they came to their view	29%
How it guides their actions	29%
The source for their stats	10%

Source: LinkedIn Poll

Indeed, the source for statistics is not what people most want to hear about. They want to understand what the stats mean to the other person and what shapes their views and actions. Rather than asking, "Where did you get that information?" we should be saying, "It sounds like that study had a powerful impact on you—what made it so important for you?" By inquiring about what the information means to someone rather than challenging the information itself, we can promote connection and understanding.

Moral Frameworks

If you feel you absolutely must present your case, you'll be more persuasive if you frame your argument in terms of their morality, not yours.[10] According to Jonathan Haidt, author of *The Righteous Mind: Why Good People Are Divided by Politics and Religion*, liberals and conservatives differ in their moral foundations, with liberals emphasizing fairness and protection from harm and conservatives focusing on loyalty, authority, and purity. We tend to craft arguments based in our own moral foundations: for example, when liberals say we should support gender-affirming care to protect transgender people from harm rather than appealing to respect for the authority of medical professionals, or when conservatives argue that free markets are foundational to national prosperity rather than highlighting opportunities for diverse entrepreneurs. We do this even when we're trying to convince someone on the other side, suggesting lack of awareness of moral frameworks of people whose values differ from our own. Try crafting arguments for your position based in the other side's morality—this is a great perspective-taking exercise and will help you to be more effective in pleading your case.

TELL YOUR STORY

Thirty years ago, abortion was my entry to reaching across the political divide. In the early 1990s, I started a Common Ground group to bring together pro-choice and pro-life people who wanted to engage in dialogue. I was angry at the pro-life activists who shouted at me and my coworkers and the patients we served as we ran the gauntlet into the doctor's office that provided abortions several days each week. I was exhausted by the endless pro-choice coalition strategizing and organizing. I felt certain that my anger and exhaustion wasn't helping the women I was trying to support.

After hearing a story on NPR about a group in St. Louis made up of pro-life and pro-choice people who were having conversations with each other, I was intrigued. I tracked them down, and they sent me materials and newspaper articles and a videotape of a news story about their project (this was pre-internet). I reached out to the director of the pro-life crisis pregnancy center in my town and shared the idea with her. She was game to give it a try, and we invited our networks to gather at the library to talk with each other.

Common Ground provided an opportunity to hear people talk about their views with authenticity and complexity. I listened to pro-life feminists and pro-choice Catholics and other varied standpoints. I agreed with some things expressed by people on "the other side," and I didn't see eye to eye with everything I heard from people whose political position presumably aligned with my own. It became obvious to me that most people's views on abortion are far more complex than either movement's labels and slogans communicate.

Common Ground was a transformational experience for me. Although it didn't change my stance on reproductive rights, it did shift my feelings about people who disagreed with me. Understanding how others came to their views helped me recognize the sensitivity and reason that informed their conclusions. People did say things that struck me as shortsighted, hypocritical, or unsympathetic; however, it was clear to me that this was true of people on my own side as well. Ultimately, listening with the intent to understand expanded my limited perception of people who disagreed with me as I came to appreciate their humanity and complexity.

I've carried that experience with me through the past several decades, into my work on LGBTQ psychology, into my work training law enforcement, into conversations about religion, the economy, diversity, and candidates for public office. Common Ground sparked my curiosity and taught me the importance of listening to people share where they're coming from. Ultimately, it set me on the trajectory that led to my work on bridging political divides.

What you've just read is my story about the power of engaging across the divide. I know that if I want to persuade you to have conversations across political disagreement, I'll be most successful if I share my personal experience. We imagine that arguments supported by facts will engender the greatest respect, but in reality, research shows that arguments embedded in stories are particularly persuasive.[11] What's more, personal stories are perceived as truer than facts because seemingly factual information can be contested in moral disagreements, whereas stories are more impervious to attack.[12]

Consider a narrative that expresses your views on a topic. Perhaps it's something that happened to you, or it could be a story you heard that had an impact on you. Is there an experience or process that you can describe with a beginning, middle, and end? Your story will be particularly memorable and convincing if it transports the listener and arouses emotion.[13] You might even try writing out your story—a side benefit is that you may gain some insight or process your feelings through the act of writing.

If you find yourself abbreviating your views into slogans, try elaborating your perspective into a story. Slogans can be effective for telegraphing solidarity with people on your own side, but they can be alienating or confusing to people who are outside your bubble. What story demonstrates that Black Lives Matter? What's the narrative underlying your desire to Make America Great Again? Ultimately, our opinions will be more compelling if we express them in stories rather than stats and slogans.

Most of us are not initially drawn to a cause due to factual information, although we may accumulate a great deal of it that supports our views as we commit to a position. In conversation, try focusing on what has shaped your views rather than the data that corroborates what you currently believe. Rather than citing levels of carbon dioxide in the atmosphere, talk about your family camping trips that fostered your love of nature. Instead of calculating the economic benefits of fracking, share your experience of being laid off from your job in the oil industry.

Stories require us to reveal our humanity, which can feel more vulnerable than debating facts. It may be uncomfortable to lay down our data and share more of ourselves, but it is so much more rewarding.

COMMUNICATING ACROSS POWER DIFFERENCES

One of the most frequent questions I receive focuses on what to do when there's an imbalance of power. How do dialogue principles and skills apply when one person is in a more powerful position than the other? You might experience this in the workplace or family relationships. On a group level, this may occur when there's a history of laws that exclude, imprison, or enslave or when access to resources, power, representation, safety, and autonomy are not equally distributed. Do you need to alter your approach to account for an uneven playing field?

First, it's important to note that determining who has more power is a challenging task. People are more likely to be aware of and identify with their disadvantages than their advantages.[14] Plus, we have multiple aspects of our identity associated with privilege or lack thereof. I experience various disadvantages as a biracial, Asian American, bisexual, Jewish, Buddhist woman. However, as a cisgender, relatively light-skinned, currently able-bodied, US-born citizen, who was raised with economic and educational resources, I experience considerable privilege. Although there's not always an obvious determination of power and powerlessness, we can try to be sensitive to heightened vulnerability that someone may be feeling due to their experiences or history individually or as part of a group of people.

If you are in a dominant position, it will be particularly important for you to use reflection to demonstrate that you hear and understand the nondominant person. In one study, White Americans who received and reflected the experiences of Mexican Americans showed the greatest change in attitudes toward Mexican Americans, whereas Mexican American's attitudes toward White Americans benefited the most when Mexican Americans had their own experiences reflected back to them. Similarly, Palestinians seem to have a greater need to share their perspectives and be listened to by Jewish Israelis than vice versa. Indeed, reflection of their experiences increased their warmth and empathy toward Israelis, whereas Israelis' attitudes toward Palestinians shifted when they were in the listening role.[15]

If you are in a situation of privilege with regard to the topic at hand, or if you hold more power than the other person, know that your curiosity puts a demand on the other person. It's possible that you haven't seen people like them represented in the media, in history classes, or in leadership of organizations, companies, and government. It's asking a lot to request that someone reveal experiences that you're unaware of due to their stigma and your privilege. When possible, try to educate yourself first, which will help you to be more knowledgeable and will reduce the risk of asking questions that reflect stereotypes.

And if you are in a conversation where you feel powerless, targeted, and marginalized, what do you do? People sometimes pose this question to me as, "Do I have to have a dialogue with someone who does not even think I should exist?" The simplest response is no, you do not have to. It's your choice; you get to decide. I do think it's useful to reflect on your goals, though. Do you want to repair, maintain, or deepen your connection or to understand them better? Are you hoping to persuade them or to find common ground? If so, you might want to have a conversation.

Also important, however, is considering how your motivations to engage in dialogue weigh in comparison to your other desires—to feel validated, to have your values mirrored back to you, to conserve your energy for other purposes. For me, this equation is not the same in every circumstance. Sometimes I have the energy to answer questions, share my stories, and learn more about why someone thinks bisexuality doesn't exist (for example). Sometimes I do not. I reflect on my available resources when these opportunities arise to guide my decisions. For me, this is preferable to a hard-and-fast rule that could either preclude me from potentially meaningful and transformative interactions or commit me to participate in every potentially draining interface.

Communicating across Power Differences

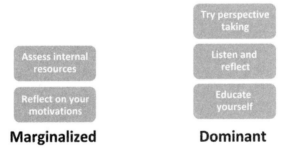

Marginalized

- Assess internal resources
- Reflect on your motivations

Dominant

- Try perspective taking
- Listen and reflect
- Educate yourself

DEEPENING CONVERSATIONS
WITH PEOPLE ON YOUR OWN SIDE

If you're repelled by the idea of listening to someone on the other side of the political divide, consider expanding your conversations with people whose politics are aligned with your own. Such exchanges often consist of confirming that the other person is on your side, conveying arguments and articles that affirm your mutual position, and venting frustration about people who disagree with your shared view. What if we went a little deeper? What if we invited them to share how they came to their views? What if we divulged experiences and values that shaped our own perspectives? What if we got curious about the complexity of people's relationship to the issues?

You may wonder what there is to gain from deeper conversations with our allies. Based on my experience, these interactions foster insight into our own and others' values, help us to refine our reasoning, and enhance our ability to articulate our perspectives. Furthermore, these novel exchanges can strengthen our ties with people in our circle. All of which can prepare us to be more effective advocates and hone the skills that will help us to communicate across differences.

I notice that people often talk as if everyone shares their perspective. By assuming everyone is on the same side, you reveal your narrow view. Even if you know someone is generally in agreement with you on an issue, they may not share your motivations, reasoning, and meaning that it holds for them. Open conversations might reveal the diversity of views in the people around you.

A FEW MORE THINGS

Even with the best of intentions, and despite the compelling evidence supporting the approaches I've described, you may have a difficult time sticking to the guidance in this chapter. Effective listening takes effort. Most people tell me it goes against their natural inclinations, especially when interacting with people who hold different values or perspectives. You may not have a relevant story at hand. Sometimes you simply want to vent or argue or walk away. Start with low stakes conversations. Some people find it easiest to try things out when there's not a prior relationship—for example, a seatmate on a plane. Others prefer to test the waters with family or friends. Either way, cut yourself some slack and expect that things won't always go smoothly.

A lot of people tell me they simply avoid talking about politics with people who they know they disagree with. It turns out, there's evidence to support this approach. Whereas talking about areas of disagreement can promote understanding, talking about a neutral topic that reveals commonalities is more effective for reducing cross-partisan animosity.[16] Consider conversations about your favorite vacation, something delicious you cooked, TV shows, or other positive subjects.

You'll be most more satisfied and less frustrated if you have appropriate expectations for engaging across political disagreement. To be honest, people on the other side of the political spectrum are unlikely to completely shift their position and adopt your view. They may, however, become less extreme and more complex in their thinking. Furthermore, you can increase your understanding of another view and generate empathy toward the other person. Your relationship can also deepen as you increase trust, caring, and warmth.

Given these parameters, what might success look like? Imagine family members who hold strong opposing views engaging in conversation with a shared goal of understanding each other. Rather than expressing forceful arguments, they ask one another how they came to their views and share their own journeys. They might react to an unsettling opinion with curiosity, not frustration. They would be unlikely to change each other's mind about policies, but they may develop more accurate and more complex views of a person who holds an opposing position. Moreover, they may mend or sustain a relationship with someone who is important in their life. They may find it easier to stay connected.

Dialogue is informative. It can help us develop a more accurate view of others by hearing their values and experiences. Dialogue is healing. It can help us to feel close to other people by understanding them and feeling understood. Dialogue is engaging. It can welcome people into meaningful exchange about important matters. In short, dialogue is an empowering practice that can help to correct our distorted perceptions, repair our ruptured relationships, and help us connect with the humanity and complexity in ourselves and others.

KEY TAKEAWAYS

- Be curious, strive to truly understand where someone else is coming from.

- Encourage elaboration by providing uninterrupted time to speak, listening, reflecting, and prompting the speaker to share more.

- Share stories, not stats and slogans.

- Be aware of power differences and adapt your approach accordingly.

- Deepen and complexify your conversations with people on your own side.

- Maintain appropriate expectations.

CHAPTER 9

Participate Meaningfully in Community and Country

The US democracy is at risk. Similar severe polarization has been observed in countries where democracy is in decline. Aspects of US systems of governance, such as the entrenched two-party system and gerrymandering, make it particularly challenging to shift out of polarized partisanship.[1] Furthermore, misperceptions of people across the political spectrum fuel antidemocratic values—the more you think the other party will violate democratic norms, the more apt you are to think your party should do the same.[2]

Are you concerned about this potential loss of our democracy, the most enduring one in history? For generations, people who lived in democracies cared a lot about the fact that their country was a democracy. Over time, people have expressed a greater willingness to give up their own power to authoritarian alternatives. Much of the shift is generational, with millennials' indifference to democracy powering this attitudinal change.[3]

I'm worried about this decline. Some key elements of a functioning democracy are election integrity and voting rights, freedom of speech and the press, and government that hinders political intimidation rather than commits it.[4] Which of these would you be willing to sacrifice?

I'm committed to shoring up rather than giving up on our system of government. Democracy is difficult and imperfect, but in my view, it's far better than the alternatives. As fraught as our country is with inefficient governance and structural inequities, we strive for a more perfect union that embodies justice, liberty, and domestic tranquility. I believe that these ideals and the institutions that support them are worth maintaining.

I feel proud of the long history of democracy in the United States, and I hate to see it undermined under my watch and yours. Political polarization is eating away at the social and institutional fabric of our country. The more divided we are, the more vulnerable we are as a collective to antidemocratic forces within and outside the United States. The work you've done so far in this book has prepared you to be part of the solution, and this chapter will offer some ideas as to how.

WE THE PEOPLE

My first act of political advocacy occurred when I was four years old—I wrote to President Nixon and asked him to stop the Vietnam War . . . and he did. The next time I got involved in politics was joining the campaign to help Barack Obama win the presidency . . . and he did. It's possible that these two events, nearly forty years apart, gave me an overinflated sense of political self-efficacy. Nonetheless, I want to share with you my confidence that if I can make a difference, so can you. In the words of President Obama, "I'm asking you to believe. Not in my ability to bring about change—but in yours."[5]

The term "democracy" was coined in ancient Greece from two words: demos ("common people") and kratos ("strength").[6] Thus, democracy is about rule of the people or empowering the members of a society. Unlike in ancient Athens, US citizens do not vote on every law; rather we elect people to do that on our behalf. Even though we don't directly weigh in on each decision, democracy works best when we participate by electing the decision makers and more.

You literally cannot spell "United States" without *U* (you) and *I* and *US*. I take this to mean that to achieve the full potential of our country, we need everyone's participation. Participatory democracy relies on the populace to take part in collective endeavors, including civic organizations and government.[7] Read on to learn about the ways you can engage and how doing so will strengthen our democracy, as well as benefit you as an individual.

VOTE

Even in a presidential election with historically high turnout, one-third of eligible voters don't participate.[8] Half or more opt out of midterm and local elections. About a fifth of US adults are eligible, but unregistered voters. Americans who don't register to vote tend to be disinterested in politics and disconnected from their community.[9] I'm saddened by the large numbers of Americans who don't participate in elections. Voting is a bedrock of democracy, and it's an important way for people to have a say in how things are run in their community and country.

People on both the political Left and Right support free and fair elections, although they may disagree about the greatest threat to our electoral system. The Left emphasizes the dangers of voter suppression, whereas the Right elevates concerns about voter fraud. Although both do occur, claims of each side are likely exaggerated.[10] Voter fraud appears to constitute a miniscule portion of any election, suggesting that we should put more energy into helping people vote than preventing them from voting. And yet, deliberate attempts to restrict specific demographic segments of voters do not seem to be the primary impediment to voting. So, what does determine whether or not people vote?

Who Votes and Why?

To vote in the United States, you must be eighteen years or older and a citizen. Depending on what state you live in, you may be barred from voting if you've had a prior felony conviction. You also need to be registered to vote, a process that differs by state. And then you actually have to vote. Older Americans, those with higher income and education, White people, and women are the most likely to vote.[11] Many people who vote do so only intermittently, so voter behavior is not just about who you are; it's also based on decisions voters make in a particular election cycle.

Voter turnout is highly correlated with the belief that the outcome of an election matters.[12] If you don't feel like it makes much of a difference which candidate wins, you're less likely to take the time to vote. The same is true if you don't feel like your vote has much of an impact. Elections can have substantial consequences for real-world issues that affect our lives. Everything from how much you pay in taxes to how you access health care to what your children learn in school is dependent on the policymakers we elect. Some national elections are decided by a few thousand votes, and the margin for local elections can be a few hundred or less. With these narrow wins, your vote can have a tremendous impact.

Similar to other human behavior, voting is affected by what the people around you are doing. If your friends and family vote, you are more likely to vote. If voting is a topic of conversation in your community or congregation or workplace, you are more likely to vote.[13] Some people I know invite friends over to complete their mail-in ballots together—not everyone has to vote the same way, but it reminds people to complete and send in their ballot. I vote early by mail and wear my "I voted" sticker (which I stuck on a button for easy reuse) every day for weeks leading up to an election as a reminder to everyone in view to vote.

Becoming an Informed Voter

Some people don't vote or don't vote on all the issues because they feel uninformed about the issues and candidates and don't know who to vote for. Nonvoters are more likely to find the abundance of information available these days overwhelming rather than informative.[14] For many years after my career brought me to Santa Barbara, I didn't know anything about what was going on in my local government—I couldn't even name any of my elected officials. Every Election Day, I would call a friend whose values I trusted and follow his guidance to complete my ballot.

Then, I got involved in the Obama campaign, which led me to volunteer for local campaigns, which motivated me to run for the local Democratic Central Committee, which involved me in the candidate endorsement process, which made me a highly informed and engaged community member. Now, every election cycle, I send out an email with my voting recommendations to several hundred people. Some people do their own research, and my email is one additional piece of information. Others tell me they bring my email with them to their polling location or complete their mail-in ballot according to my endorsements. It puts me in a weirdly powerful position, a responsibility I take very seriously. I research the candidates and ballot measures, and I make sure to provide a recommendation for every item on the ballot, knowing that, if someone pauses to figure out how to vote on a local seat or ballot measure or judge, the uncompleted ballot might get buried in the stack of mail and not get sent in. As

Election Day approaches, if I haven't sent it out yet, friends start asking when they'll get my recommendations.

You may not have time or feel well enough informed to become the point person for voter recommendations among your friends (although if you choose to take up the mantle, you too could become a weirdly powerful person). However, if you're not sure how to vote on certain ballot items, you might try to identify someone in your network who can provide guidance. If not a personal contact, try to identify a political party or non-partisan organization (such as the League of Women Voters) that aligns with your interests or values, and see if they have recommendations—they might even host a forum you can attend to hear directly from local candidates. And if you happen to live in Santa Barbara County, let me know, and I would be happy to put you on my list!

Overcoming Barriers to Voting

The logistics of voting can have a differential impact on various groups of people. For example, some cite not having enough time to register or vote as a reason they don't participate in elections,[15] which may be especially influential for people who have little control over their work schedules. Young adults and those in unstable housing situations may find it challenging to re-register every time they move. Lack of civic infrastructure, such as broadband internet access and public gathering spaces, is associated with low voter turnout in rural areas.[16]

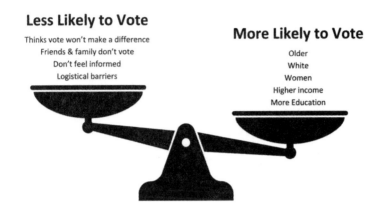

Less Likely to Vote

Thinks vote won't make a difference
Friends & family don't vote
Don't feel informed
Logistical barriers

More Likely to Vote

Older
White
Women
Higher income
More Education

To be sure, structural barriers limit voting in a wide variety of ways, making it more difficult in some states or counties for citizens to register to vote, to receive a ballot, or to get to the polls. Requirements for government-issued ID, long lines at polling locations, and limited voting periods can be impediments to participation in elections. Although some solutions to low voter turnout need to be enacted by elected officials at the national and state level, every eligible voter can participate by doing the following:

1. Register to vote, and re-register if you move. Contact your county elections office if you need help.

2. Figure out who and what you want to vote for. Seek information from trusted sources if you want guidance.

3. Make a plan. If you identify when and where you vote, as well as what you will be doing immediately before you vote, you're much more likely to follow through with

your intention.[17] Make sure you know how you'll get your ballot (by mail or at the polls), where to return it, and by when. Contact your county elections office if you need help.

4. Vote. Keeping in mind the potential logistical barriers to voting, vote as early as possible. If you run into a problem getting a ballot or having it accepted, fill out a provisional ballot and/or contact your county elections office.

SUPPORT ELECTIONS

Because I am engaged in politics, people often ask me what I think the outcome will be for various races. I respond, "I don't make predictions; I make phone calls!" I find that the best remedy for concern about elections is to get involved. Some of my friends seem to recognize that this is my stance, and they have stopped telling me about their election anxiety because they know I will tell them what they can do to participate. I realize engaging in elections is not everyone's cup of tea, but if you're excited, or even curious, about how to do so, read on!

After the 2000 presidential election uncertainties (remember hanging chads?), I decided to volunteer to work at the polls. It turns out they even pay you a little, so it's not technically volunteering. I received training, and I must have done well because they put me in charge of a precinct. I took the day off from work and spent Election Day overseeing the process of voters receiving and returning ballots. It was exciting to play an active role in our democracy! I learned so much about voting, and the experience made me feel confident about voting procedures in my county. If this sounds like something you might like to do, contact your county elections office—they're usually looking for people to help out!

Another way to participate is talking to voters on behalf of a political party, candidate, ballot measure, or cause you support. People are more likely to vote if someone asks them to do it; voter contact helps people feel like their vote matters.[18] You might balk at the idea of knocking on doors or calling voters, thinking you would be arguing with people who disagree with you. In fact, that would be a terrible waste of time and energy on the part of the campaign. In reality, these conversations typically focus on identifying voters who are likely to support your candidate or issue (voter ID) and then getting out the vote (GOTV), which may include providing information about polling locations and reminders about deadlines. Less commonly, voter contact focuses on trying to convince someone to vote in a certain way. Even voter persuasion is nonconfrontational, sometimes discussing a candidate's voting record or using "deep canvassing" to engage the voter in a conversation to learn about their values and share stories.[19]

My friend Darcél Elliott, who has canvassed and coordinated volunteers for countless campaigns, shared with me her experience, which resonates with my own. She noted, "Direct voter contact can be a wonderful way to counteract some of the more contentious rhetoric pushed by mass media. Having conversations face-to-face, or even by phone, makes it very clear that the over-whelming majority of average, everyday voters are even-tempered, just like us in terms of demeanor, and frequently even grateful for another human being reaching out to them to educate them about what will be on the ballot and how to vote."

PARTICIPATE IN GOVERNMENT

Do you have a question or an opinion you want to share with an elected official? There are many avenues for communicating with representatives. You can typically find contact information or a form you can fill out on their website (see https://www.house.gov/representatives for congressional representatives' websites). National and state representatives also typically have a district office, in addition to an office in the state capitol or Washington, DC. Whichever office you contact, you're more likely to reach a staff member rather than the elected official. Don't be disappointed if you end up communicating with a staff member—these professionals handle constituent services and advise the representatives on policy matters. I have found staff to be responsive and accessible. Even if you call and leave a voicemail, that gives your representative some idea of what their constituents think about an issue.

It's helpful to know which matters are handled by the various levels of government so you know whom to contact about policies such as immigration (federal), criminal justice (state), or public safety (local), although some issues, such as schools, have aspects that cut across these levels. National issues may receive the most press coverage, but there are vital issues that are decided at the state and local levels, and Americans tend to trust local and state government.[20] Local government is quite broad and includes county, city, school district, and special districts that govern specific services, such as water.

You can go a step further and become part of government. States and municipalities maintain appointed committees, boards, and commissions. These groups consist of community members who provide guidance, make recommendations, allocate funds, and organize programs and other functions. To find out about vacancies, see if this information is on a website or contact your government or an elected official's office.

Have you ever thought about running for office? I joke that elected office is the job with the most expensive and complicated interview process. If you're thinking about becoming a candidate, I suggest you follow the guidance in this chapter about supporting elections and participating in government. There's also a lot to learn about campaign strategy, endorsements, fundraising, and the issues. You can find a tremendous amount of information online—start by doing a search for "how to run for office."

OTHER WAYS TO ENGAGE IN COMMUNITY AND COUNTRY

In Chapter 3, I recommended creating some boundaries around social media usage. When you disengage from technology, it offers you more time to engage with actual human beings. Involvement in community organizations, including faith congregations, has declined over many decades.[21] This is unfortunate since these institutions build social connections and promote civic engagement.[22] Also, volunteering is good for you; it's associated with better health and well-being.[23]

Furthermore, reduced interaction with Americans of differing backgrounds and values erodes social trust and exacerbates polarization.[24] The more you interact with actual humans, the less you rely on stereotypes of people on the other side. There are many ways to work together toward shared goals, such as coaching soccer, participating in a community cleanup, and assisting people in hospice, shelters, and disasters. You can volunteer to help at fundraisers or usher at cultural events to add some social and cultural experiences into the mix. Nonprofit organizations are often seeking board members with leadership, organizational, and financial skills.

You might choose to be part of a movement, to join with others who are advocating for a cause you care about. Activism can be a very meaningful endeavor that aligns with your values. However, social media activism is neither effective nor as beneficial as civic participation. You will be most powerful if you use the opportunity to engage with other people directly, working together toward collective goals.

National service, both military and civilian, offers an opportunity for people of different backgrounds to serve a common purpose. Such intergroup contact can encourage positive relationships across diversity, including race, gender, and religion.[25]

One argument for a national service requirement is to promote social cohesion across ideological and other differences.[26] National service, like the military, the Peace Corps, VISTA, and others, also exposes participants to unfamiliar regions of the country and the world and instills the value of public service.

As you can see, there are a multitude of ways to participate in community and country. You can be indoors or outdoors, in your local community or across the world, supporting causes, people, animals, nature, and other things you value. Engaging in these ways will benefit yourself, as well as others.

E PLURIBUS UNUM

You learned in Part I of this book that baseball was my entry into sports fandom. Sitting in the stands has given me a lot of time to reflect on the sport, and I've come to see ways in which baseball is so incredibly American. Just like individual states, each player has their own talents, shortcomings, and personality. Fans might be drawn to a particular team member based on their performance at bat or in the field, or they may like their swagger, bushy beard, or the causes they support. So, each player is distinct, but they also work together. As a team, their diverse talents are a strength. You don't need everyone to be a good pitcher, but you need a few players who are. Similarly, each state in our union has a distinct geographic landscape, industry, history, and culture. In baseball, the focus is sometimes on the individual, and sometimes it's about how the team operates together. Just like the United States.

That's how baseball led me to reflect on the name of our country, the "United States." Our country is made up of fifty states and a number of territories, with their own names and industries and cultures and histories. Some have major urban centers, others are more rural and agricultural, and some are a mix of both. Even the way we speak belies our origins. I grew up in Virginia, and though most of my southern accent has disappeared, I refuse to give up "y'all." People from other parts of the country denote the second person plural with "you" or "youse" or "you guys." Our home state or the state where we live may have particular meaning for us, for our identity, for our people.

Each state is unique, yet we are bound together as a country. We are united states. This is not just a little idea somewhere down on the list of priorities—it's our name. Historically, maintaining power at the state level has some problematic origins in slavery.[27] I believe, however, that history is not the only basis for people wanting their state to have a voice beyond themselves as an individual. I hear people in California making a case against the Electoral College by saying they don't want people in Wyoming having so much of a say in who runs our country. I'm fairly certain that people in Wyoming don't want Californians overpowering their voice either. We have a connection to our state, and we want that distinct position taken into account in the federal government.

The traditional motto of the United States, *e pluribus unum*, means "out of many, one." We are a country of many states and territories. Our families took many paths to live on this land. We represent many cultures, faiths, and traditions. Many values, ideologies, and priorities guide us. And we are one country. Somehow, we need to commit to one another, to knit our manys together into one. The more I view the oneness across the wide range of Americans, the more patriotic I feel.

Although leaders can do their part to foster harmony, there is much we can each do in service of bringing our country together. We can participate meaningfully in community and country, and we can approach every interaction as an opportunity to revitalize our connections. Our diversity is a strength; we don't need to set aside our differences, but we do need to approach each other with curiosity, respect, and generosity of spirit.

Ultimately, your participation in community and country will strengthen our democracy and the social fabric of our country.

I suspect it may also embellish your own sense of optimism, pride, and agency. I hope you will join me in healing and fortifying our country.

KEY TAKEAWAYS

- Political polarization contributes to the decline of democracy, and civic engagement supports democracy.

- You will be most likely to vote if you are registered, feel informed, believe your vote makes a difference, and have a voting plan.

- You can support elections by working at the polls and talking with voters.

- There are many ways to participate in government, including communicating with elected officials, serving in appointed positions, and running for office.

- Community engagement and national service benefit the individual, as well as the collective.

- Coming together across our differences will help us reach the promise of our country.

CHAPTER 10

Join the Bridging Movement

I'm in a Zoom breakout room with three other people. We are introducing ourselves. Jeff provides a pro-democracy pathway to reducing polarization through the Interactivity Foundation. Kristin is with the Civic Health Project, which amplifies organizations and individuals who are engaged in cross-partisan work. Brian's Citizen Connect online platform provides resources to support bridge-building efforts. And me? I'm a professor who wrote a book and gives talks and workshops about dialogue across political lines. My work feels small in comparison to the national organizations these people represent, but it was enough to get me invited to the #ListenFirst Coalition Zoom meeting, and for that I am grateful.

Started in 2017 by four bridging organizations (Listen First Project, Village Square, Living Room Conversations, and National Institute for Civil Discourse), the #ListenFirst Coalition now consists of over 500 groups. Coming together monthly on Zoom to share, learn, empower, support, and network with each other, the Coalition seeks to "build a new foundation of trust and grace upon which shared humanity is recognized, violence is avoided, division doesn't sell, common challenges are solved, and differences make our democracy and society healthy, robust and resilient."[1]

Each Coalition partner plays a role individually in helping to reduce polarization, build social cohesion, and shore up our democracy—but together they represent an even stronger force for change. The #ListenFirst Coalition is the heartbeat of the bridging movement, pumping information, encouragement, and support to a vast network of organizations that are working hard to heal our country.

These Zoom meetings started in the lead-up to the 2020 election, during the contentious Biden-Trump contest, around the same time *Beyond Your Bubble* was published. After developing resources in relative isolation, I found it restorative to connect with others who were bridging the political divide. It is encouraging to know that a large community of people is dedicated to harnessing accurate information and human connection to support civil discourse and democracy.

Many people are not aware of the bridging movement. As detailed in Chapter 2, the media leans into covering controversy rather than cooperation. When I tell people what I'm seeing in the bridging movement, most are interested and heartened. So, whether or not you choose to join in, you may benefit by simply knowing about it.

SOME GREAT INITIATIVES

Numerous bridging initiatives uplift my spirit and influence my thinking. I'll share a few here, as well as point you to additional resources later in the chapter. Trust me, there are so many more than what I have room to describe here in this book. This is simply a glimpse into a multifaceted movement of creative and committed Americans.

Braver Angels

In May 2022, during a feverish time in the national conversation on abortion, I attended a Braver Angels online debate about the topic. Over 150 people participated, representing a wide range of views. Braver Angels debates are highly structured and skillfully moderated. The format encourages thoughtful consideration of controversial topics and prevents the conversation from devolving into conflict. With courage and vulnerability, people volunteered to share their experiences and perspectives. I was glad to see the collective express respect and support verbally and nonverbally. In contrast to what is often represented in media and social media, every speaker articulated complex and caring views.

Online debates are but one dimension of Braver Angels' work. They offer workshops, e-courses, a podcast, conversation guides, and events, with the mission to "bring Americans together to bridge the partisan divide and strengthen our democratic republic."[2] Their diverse approaches are a strength of their organization as people can plug into the organization's activities and resources at whatever level fits their time and interests. Their workshop model—built on identifying commonalities and building empathy—has been shown to reduce partisan animosity.[3] Furthermore, their events, network of organizations, and local alliances cultivate connection.

In 2023, Braver Angels hosted a convention in Gettysburg, Pennsylvania, on the anniversary of the Civil War battle that took place there. The convention consisted of equal numbers of delegates who lean Red and lean Blue. Attendees engaged together to articulate and commit to principles of civic renewal, echoing President Abraham Lincoln's aspiration that "this government of the people, by the people, for the people, shall not perish from the earth."[4] I find Braver Angels' dedication to engaging Americans from both sides of the partisan divide visionary and inspiring.

Braver Angels is one of many organizations that brings people together across ideological differences. You can look to #ListenFirst Coalition partners for additional ideas.

Bridging Divides & Strengthening Democracy

In September 2022, I attended a conference called "Bridging Divides & Strengthening Democracy: From Science to Practice." This virtual forum was the culmination of a competition to develop and test strategies to reduce partisan animosity and decrease support for undemocratic processes. The organizers put out a call to researchers, received 252 entries, and tested the interventions in a well-controlled online environment with a large sample.[5]

As a researcher, I was impressed with the rigor of the science, but what really caught my attention were the results. Remarkably, of the twenty-five interventions they tested, almost every single one was effective in reducing partisan animosity![6] Many strategies focused on correcting misperceptions—participants were surprised to learn that people on the other side agreed with them on some things, did not support undemocratic processes, and were willing to learn about another perspective. Other approaches humanized people across the political spectrum by showing them sharing struggles, collaborating, and talking about aspects of themselves that were misunderstood.

These findings are extremely encouraging. With tools that can reduce partisan animosity, we may be more willing to connect across political disagreement and shift the spiraling polarization that strains our relationships and our democratic processes. The science is advancing, as researchers and practitioners partner to continue testing the effectiveness of strategies identified in the first phase.

This is but one example of harnessing research to address political polarization. The citations I've provided throughout this book demonstrate the wealth of investigative energy and research findings that help to guide bridging efforts.

Government Initiatives

Given public divisiveness among politicians, I feel more optimistic knowing that elected officials are working across the aisle. In the US Congress, the Problem Solvers Caucus is composed of equal numbers of Democratic and Republican representatives. They work together to "champion ideas that appeal to a broad spectrum of the American people."[7] I am proud that my congressional representative is a member of the caucus, and I make sure to communicate my appreciation to him. It's also exciting that, under Utah governor Spencer Cox's leadership, the National Governors Association is taking up the mantle with their Disagree Better Initiative. Furthermore, when I've been invited to provide training on bridging political divides for state legislators and local political parties, it's been well received. Although we may hear primarily about divisiveness and gridlock, policymakers are part of the bridging movement. When advocates with opposing agendas cooperate to identify common ground, it makes it easier for legislation to be supported across both sides of the aisle.[8]

One bipartisan initiative that would specifically support bridging efforts is the Building Civic Bridges Act (BCBA), a bill that was introduced into Congress in 2022 (and, as of this writing, has not yet become law). The BCBA would establish an Office of Civic Bridgebuilding to support research, provide training for AmeriCorps members in bridge-building techniques, administer grants to support bridge-building efforts, and convene and coordinate bridging movement activities. I love the idea of the US government taking this role to heal our country, much as we invest in supporting conflict resolution in other parts of the world. I encourage you to contact your congressional representative and ask them to support the BCBA.

In September 2023, thirteen US presidential centers issued a joint statement in support of democracy. This remarkable show of unity belies both the threat to our democracy and a commitment to the ideals of our country that crosses party lines. This passage particularly resonates with me and with the message of this book, that we the people are called to rise to our potential in the face of political polarization: "Each of us has a role to play and responsibilities to uphold. Our elected officials must lead by example and govern effectively in ways that deliver for the American people. This, in turn, will help to restore trust in public service. The rest of us must engage in civil dialogue; respect democratic institutions and rights; uphold safe, secure, and accessible elections; and contribute to local, state, or national improvement."[9]

THINGS YOU CAN DO (MOST OF WHICH REQUIRE VERY LITTLE EFFORT)

Have I piqued your interest? Do you want to know more or get involved? Here, I offer some suggestions for what you can do. It's okay if you don't have time for a big commitment; you can still tap into the resources of the bridging movement to boost your knowledge of what's going on and your optimism for the future of our country. And if you do decide to get involved, I'm guessing engaging with the bridgers will support everything you've learned in this book: reducing polarizing input, building individual capacity, and strengthening connections.

Sign up to receive a weekly or monthly email. Literally, just sign up; you don't even have to read it. But when it shows up in your inbox, you will remember that there's a bridging movement, and when you want to be uplifted by what's happening in the movement, all you have to do is open an email to get a shot of optimistic action.

- I highly recommend the weekly Listen First Friday emails, which you can get by signing the Listen First pledge (https://www.listenfirstproject.org/pledge).

- If you've made it this far into the book, I'll take that as a sign that you might like to hear more from me. I share thoughts and resources in my monthly email newsletter (https://taniaisrael.com/newsletter/).

- Choose a bridging organization that interests you and sign up for their newsletter. You can find a lot of options on the Citizen Connect website (https://citizenconnect .us/organizations/).

Listen to a podcast. I love having bridgers in my ears while I cook, walk, and drive. You can find some great listening options through The Democracy Group, a network of podcasts about democracy, civic engagement, and civil discourse (https:// www.democracygroup.org/). Here are a few podcasts I find particularly enlightening:

- *A Braver Way*—hosted by Mónica Guzmán, founder of Braver Angels, this podcast features interviews and demonstrations of conversations that bridge divides. https://braverangels.org/abraverway/

- *Let's Find Common Ground*—Richard Davies and Ashley Milne-Tyte's podcast sheds light on paths out of polarization through interviews with leaders and experts. https://commongroundcommittee.org/podcasts/

- *Civil Squared*—although it no longer creates new content, the fifty-six-episode archive is an informative resource that elevates civil discourse. https://civilsquared.org/listen/

Follow bridgers on social media. Whereas many people complain that their Twitter/X feeds are filled with partisan hate, mine consists of resources for bridge-building efforts, announcements about opportunities for dialogue, and encouraging research findings. In addition to the many organizations you can follow, you might also enjoy following individual bridgers, such as Manu Meel (@ManuMeel_), John Wood Jr. (@JohnRWoodJr), and me (@taniaisraelphd).

Participate in a bridging activity. Perhaps you're already embracing opportunities to engage in conversations across political differences at family gatherings or in line at the supermarket, but if you're seeking opportunities for dialogue and other opportunities to strengthen connections, civic engagement, and democracy, here are some great options:

- Citizen Connect is a rich repository for bridging movement events. Search the calendar to find an activity that interests you. https://citizenconnect.us/events/

- National Week of Conversation is hosted by the #ListenFirst Coalition and offers a wide range of programming from many organizations. With so many opportunities offered during the week, it's a great time to discover what the bridging movement has to offer! https://conversation.us/

- Braver Angels brings Americans together across the partisan divide through many means. You can attend virtual events, join a local alliance, view past debates, and more. https://braverangels.org

- Living Room Conversations provides opportunities to join or host conversations and offers resources to help people connect. https://livingroomconversations.org/

- The Polarization Detox Challenge is a four-week program that you can accomplish in just five minutes per day. Built on evidence and designed to support people who want to depolarize, this is a great self-guided activity. https://startswith.us/pdc/

- One Small Step brings strangers together across different political views. You can sign up to participate and/or hear the conversations other pairs recorded. https://storycorps.org/discover/onesmallstep/

- *Dialogue Lab: America* is a fantastic film that chronicles a social experiment bringing together strangers across many types of diversity. If you're not ready to jump into an activity (or as an accompaniment to doing so), you can get inspired by watching other people bridge the divide. https://ideosinstitute.org/dla

Do something for an organization. You can seek opportunities to volunteer within an organization that's dedicated to bridging divides. Alternatively, you can bring bridging activities into an organization that has some other focus. I love to see all the national and local associations, congregations, campuses, and other groups embracing opportunities to bring people together across differences. Many draw on the #ListenFirst Coalition organizations for guidance and support.

HOPE

People often ask me how I can be so optimistic in the face of hostility, media bias, and seemingly irrational behavior by our fellow Americans. As a public speaker, author, psychologist, and professor, who works on bridging political divides, I am invited into many types of conversations, convenings, conferences, and communities where people want to address problems related to polarization. I interact with people of faith, lawyers, researchers, mental health professionals, elected officials, college students, and corporate employees, among others.

I have also met wonderful people in the bridging movement, fellow Americans dedicated to reducing polarization, who share my faith that we can heal our country. Linking arms with them, I feel more capable of making a contribution to achieving these goals.

By doing this work, I get a glimpse into what most media is not showing, a growing movement of Americans who are reaching across partisan divides to strengthen our skills, our connections, and our democracy. And this makes me very optimistic!

I wonder if you will think my optimism naïve, if you will dismiss all the encouragement I offer, if you will find cynicism a safer harbor. But I hope you will not. Because hope is essential. Hope will motivate you to make an effort, and it will help you to persist when the journey is difficult. Hope will even make you mentally and physically healthier.[10]

I am so filled with hope. In writing this chapter, I literally moved myself to tears reflecting on all the amazing work I've witnessed in the bridging movement. It brings to mind this quote from Barack Obama: "The best way to not feel hopeless is to get up and do something. Don't wait for good things to happen to you. If you go out and make some good things happen, you will fill the world with hope, you will fill yourself with hope." My wish is that learning about the bridging movement stirs hope within you and offers you a path for stoking the ember of hope into a flame.

Ready to Be Strong

In this book, you have been introduced to a process for navigating the challenges of living in a divided nation. It looks something like this:

Ideally, you have lowered the volume and skew of polarizing input, you feel more capable of facing challenges with humility and compassion, and your relationships are stronger. Having shifted out of the battle of political polarization, where does that leave you?

According to the musical *RENT*, the opposite of war isn't peace; it's creation. If you are not investing energy in political polarization or being jostled about by it, what can you create? What can you write, sing, say, paint, envision, teach, or learn? What kind of connections can you forge in your family, community, classroom, workplace, and yourself? What kind of country can we create together?

Political polarization could be the motivation that strengthens our minds, emotions, relationships, and democracy. It may be the catalyst for us to realize our individual and collective potential.

The word "potential" has two root meanings: possible and powerful. The first denotes capacity to become, or what one can be, but has not yet actualized. The second speaks to force, energy, capability. This journey is about actualizing your power, bringing to fruition your strong, capable self.

Despite detrimental consequences, political polarization can be difficult to resist. It feels like the news, social media, elected officials, and social movements are conspiring to keep us at a heightened state of outrage. Powerful entities profit from our distress as we feed off controversial news stories, repost antagonistic messages, and donate to candidates who rile up our fear and anger. We may feel powerless to regain control of our emotions, our communities, and our democracy.

Fortunately, there are tools that will help us navigate political polarization with our health and relationships intact. In fact, if we embrace the opportunity to develop these skills, we will actually come out stronger in the end. We will be better equipped to resolve conflicts of everyday life, to move through emotional distress, and to find our way through information overload. We will be more confident in ourselves and each other. If we choose to take on leadership roles, we will be prepared to solve the problems of our communities, our campuses, our corporations, and our country. The thing is we need to believe these tools will help and (this is the hard part) we need to use them. You may be at a crossroad, on a precipice of action, but have you yet committed to it?

Throughout this book, I've shared stories to help guide us through the process. Now, we're at the end of the book. Where are our heroes at the end of their journeys? Rocky doesn't win the battle he thought he was fighting; rather he strengthens himself and his relationships. Moana is leading her people out of the bubble they were trapped in. Dorothy is returning home, more resilient and connected.

Where are you at the end of our journey together? What's your story about yourself, about people across the political spectrum, about your capacity to navigate these polarized times?

No, wait, don't tell me yet . . . I have one more story to tell. It's the story of a young woman who saved the world . . . a lot. She is a constant source of inspiration to me. She is Buffy, the Vampire Slayer, titular character of the TV series that ran from 1997 to 2003.

According to Slayer lore, the first Slayer was created thousands of years ago by a group known as the Shadow Men, who mystically imbued a mortal girl with the essence of a demon so that she would have the supernatural strength to fight and protect them from the forces of darkness that walked the earth. When the first Slayer died, another one rose to take her place—and so on for thousands of years.

For six seasons, we hear about Buffy being the Chosen One. We learn there are many potential Slayers in the world, but only when a Slayer dies does a potential Slayer become *the* Slayer, and then that Slayer is the Chosen One. Until the end of the series.

Spoiler alert for the series finale of *Buffy the Vampire Slayer*

The world is facing darkness that Buffy cannot defeat on her own. In a final battle, heroes fight alongside former foes to combat a force that seems too powerful to overcome. Buffy needs all the potential Slayers to rise to their Slayer calling and stand with her.

This is how I feel right now. Having strengthened myself with knowledge, humility, compassion, and interpersonal connections, I poured what I have learned into this book as an offering to you and to our country. I tapped into ancient wisdom, current research, and a network of colleagues and compatriots to forge sustenance and tools for your journey. You have what you need to navigate political polarization, but only you can choose to realize your potential. Our collective powers are essential to face the challenges of our political polarization. As I learned from Buffy, only together can we save the world.

Which brings me to a quote from the final episode of *Buffy the*

Vampire Slayer. With an apocalypse looming, Buffy finds a way to empower other women with the same strength she has so they can all fight together against the dark forces Buffy can't conquer on her own. She commits her fate to be their fates, if they choose it, in a rousing call to action:

> So, here's the part where you make a choice. What if you could have that power, now?
>
> I say my power . . . should be our power. . . . From now on, every girl in the world who might be a Slayer, will be a Slayer. Every girl who could have the power, will have the power, can stand up, will stand up. Slayers . . . every one of us. Make your choice. Are you ready to be strong?[1]

So, here's the part where *you* make a choice. What if you could have the power to cultivate peace of mind and an open heart, experience only the beneficial aspects of social media, maintain connections with people who have a wide range of experiences and views, be adequately and accurately informed, and participate effectively in our democracy? Would you do it?

We may think we have no power, that media corporations, social media platforms, and elected officials are the only ones who can resolve political conflict. I say we recognize our own power. From now on, everyone who could have the capacity, will have the capacity, can stand up, will stand up, empowered, every one of us. Make your choice. Are you ready to be strong?

Acknowledgments

This book was inspired by those of you who sought my guidance and kept reminding me that I had more to offer. I am grateful that you drew this book out of me with your curiosity and thoughtful engagement at presentations, interviews, and random social interactions.

A dream team helped me bring this project to fruition. Pema Rocker came through once again as story charmer, friend, and editor extraordinaire. Matt Knauer deserves an award for his patience, loving support, and incisive feedback. Social media goddess, coach, and Canva queen, Claudia Arnett, gently nudged me forward. Ivonne Prieto Rose furnished stylistic, legal, and Dharmic guidance. I am deeply indebted to you all.

Stalwart writing buddies kept me company and kept me on track. Deanna Lee traversed the globe and many time zones via WhatsApp for daily writing sessions. Lisa Bass composed poetry and snack plates during our writing time. Alan Watt created the

100-word-per-day writing challenge at exactly the right moment and consistently reminded me that stories are a powerful vehicle for communication.

Generous friends talked through ideas, forwarded articles, and helped me maintain life balance. Appreciation to Lisa Slavid, Laury Oaks, Linda Croyle, Lori Guynes, Heather Stevenson, Marc Ostfield, Brian Julius, Stephanie Langsdorf, Aunt Judy, and Uncle Steve, among others.

Subject matter experts offered brilliant feedback and made sure I didn't embarrass myself as I ventured into topics outside my primary areas of expertise. Many thanks to Deanna Lee (Chapter 2), Merrill Morris (Chapter 2), Starshine Rochelle (Chapter 2), Claudia Arnett (Chapter 3), Josh Goodman (Chapter 3), Hunter Gelbach (Chapters 4 and 6), Linda Croyle (Chapter 5), Erika Felix (Chapter 5), Don Davis (Chapter 6), Ivonne Prieto Rose (Chapter 7), Darcél Elliott (Chapter 9), Mónica Guzmán (Chapter 10), and Kara Jarzynski (Chapter 10).

Finally, I want to thank Greenleaf Book Group for partnering with me to get this book into the world with all due speed in order to have the greatest benefit during a challenging time.

Notes

Introduction

1. American Psychological Association. "Stress in America™ 2020." https://www.apa.org/news/press/releases/stress/2020/report-october.

2. Homans, C., and McFadden, A. "Today's Politics Divide Parties, and Friends and Families, Too." *New York Times*, October 18, 2022. https://www.nytimes.com/2022/10/18/us/politics/political-division-friends-family.html.

3. Cox, D. "The State of American Friendship: Change, Challenges, and Loss." Survey Center on American Life, June 8, 2021. https://www.americansurveycenter.org/research/the-state-of-american-friendship-change-challenges-and-loss/.

4. Wikipedia. (n.d.). "1977 Nestlé Boycott." https://en.wikipedia.org/wiki/1977_Nestl%C3%A9_boycott.

Part I

1. Duhigg, C. *The Power of Habit: Why We Do What We Do in Life and Business.* New York: Random House, 2014.

2. Andreatta, B. *Wired to Resist: The Brain Science of Why Change Fails and a New Model for Driving Success.* 7th Mind Publishing, 2017.

3. Milkman, K. *How to Change: The Science of Getting from Where You Are to Where you Want to Be.* New York: Portfolio/Penguin, 2021.

Chapter 1

1. Klein, E. *Why We're Polarized.* New York: Avid Reader Press, 2020; Coleman, P. T. *The Way Out: How to Overcome Toxic Polarization.* New York: Columbia University Press, 2021.

2. Pew Research Center. "The Partisan Divide on Political Values Grows Even Wider." October 5, 2017. https://www.pewresearch.org/politics/2017/10/05/the-partisan-divide-on-political-values-grows-even-wider/.

3. Pew Research Center. "Political Polarization and the American Public." June 12, 2014. https://www.pewresearch.org/politics/2014/06/12/political-polarization-in-the-american-public/; Coleman, *The Way Out.*

4. Huff, I. "QAnon Beliefs Have Increased Since 2021 as Americans Are Less Likely to Reject Conspiracies." PRRI, June 24, 2022. https://www.prri.org/spotlight/qanon-beliefs-have-increased-since-2021-as-americans-are-less-likely-to-reject-conspiracies/.

5. Keifer, E. (2017). "'Til Trump Do Us Part: The Relationship Deal Breaker We Never Saw Coming." *Refinery29*, July 2017. https://www.refinery29.com/en-us/2017/07/162856/talking-politics-with-partner-relationship-advice.

6. Iyengar, S., Lelkes, Y., Levendusky, M., Malhotra, N., and Westwood, S., J. "The Origins and Consequences of Affective Polarization in the United States." *Annual Review of Political Science* 22, no. 1 (2019): 129–146. https://doi.org/10.1146/annurev-polisci-051117-073034.

7. Iyengar, Lelkes et al. "Origins and Consequences of Affective Polarization."

8. Pew Research Center. "As Partisan Hostility Grows, Signs of Frustration with the Two-Party System." August 9, 2022. https://www.pewresearch.org/politics/2022/08/09/as-partisan-hostility-grows-signs-of-frustration-with-the-two-party-system/.

Notes

9. Vavrek, L. "A Measure of Identity: Are You Wedded to Your Party?" *New York Times*, January 31, 2017. https://www.nytimes.com/2017/01/31/upshot/are-you-married-to-your-party.html; Iyengar, Lelkes et al. "Origins and Consequences of Affective Polarization."

10. Enders, A. M. "Issues versus Affect: How Do Elite and Mass Polarization Compare?" *The Journal of Politics* 83, no. 4 (2021). https://www.journals.uchicago.edu/doi/10.1086/715059.

11. Westfall, J., Van Boven, L., Chambers, J.R., and Judd, C.M. "Perceiving Political Polarization in the United States." *Perspectives on Psychological Science* 10 (2015): 145–158.

12. Hawkins, S., Yukdin, D., Juan-Torres, M., and Dixon, T. "Hidden Tribes: A Study of America's Polarized Landscape." More in Common, 2018. https://hiddentribes.us/media/qfpekz4g/hidden_tribes_report.pdf.

13. Starts With Us. "American Values Poll." 2023. https://startswith.us/wp-content/uploads/Report-and-Methodology-For-Website.pdf.

14. Pasek, M.H., Ankori-Karlinsky, L.O., Levy-Vene, A., and Moore-Berg, S.L. "Misperceptions about Out-Partisans' Democratic Values May Erode Democracy." *Scientific Reports* 12, no. 1 (2022): 16284. https://doi.org/10.1038/s41598-022-19616-4.

15. Yudkin, D., Hawkins, S., and Dixon, T. "The Perception Gap: How False Impressions Are Pulling Americans Apart." More in Common, 2019. https://perceptiongap.us/.

16. Ahler, D., and Sood, G. "The Parties in Our Heads: Misperceptions about Party Composition and Their Consequences." *The Journal of Politics* 80, no. 3 (2018): 964–981.

17. Moore-Berg, S. L., Ankori-Karlinsky, L., Hameiri, B., and Bruneau, E. "Exaggerated Meta-Perceptions Predict Intergroup Hostility between American Political Partisans." *Proceedings of the National Academy of Sciences* 117, no. 26 (2020): 14864–14872. https://doi.org/10.1073/pnas.2001263117.

18. Druckman, J. N., Klar, S., Krupnikov, Y., Levendusky, M., and Ryan, J. B. "(Mis)estimating Affective Polarization." *The Journal of Politics* 84, no. 2 (2022): 1106–1117. https://doi.org/10.1086/715603.

19. Klar, S., Krupnikov, Y., and Ryan, J. B. "Affective Polarization or Partisan Disdain? Untangling a Dislike for the Opposing Party from a Dislike of Partisanship." *Public Opinion Quarterly* 82, no. 2 (2018): 379–390. https://doi.org/10.1093/poq/nfy014.

20. Murray, M. "'Downhill,' 'Divisive': American Sour on Nation's Direction in New NBC Poll." NBC News, 2022. https://www.nbcnews.com/politics/meet-the-press/downhill-divisive-americans-sour-nation-s-direction-new-nbc-news-n1287888.

21. Friedman, W., and Schleifer, D. "America's Hidden Common Ground on Overcoming Divisiveness: Charting a Path Forward." Public Agenda, 2021. https://publicagenda.org/wp-content/uploads/HCG-Overcoming-Divisiveness-2021.pdf.

22. Hartman, R., Blakey, W., Womick, J. et al. "Interventions to Reduce Partisan Animosity." *Nature Human Behavior* 6 (2022): 1194–1205. https://doi.org/10.1038/s41562-022-01442-3.

23. Dimock, M., and Wike, R. "America Is Exceptional in the Nature of Its Political Divide." Pew Research Center, November 13, 2020. https://www.pewresearch.org/short-reads/2020/11/13/america-is-exceptional-in-the-nature-of-its-political-divide/.

24. Chua, A. *Political Tribes: Group Instinct and the Fate of Nations.* New York: Penguin, 2018; Brooks, A. C. *Love Your Enemies: How Decent People Can Save America from the Culture of Contempt.* New York: Broadside Books, 2019; Coleman, *The Way Out.*

Chapter 2

1. Napoli, L. *Up All Night: Ted Turner, CNN, and the Birth of 24-Hour News.* New York: Abrams, 2020.

2. Abernathy, P. M. *The State of Local News: The 2023 Report.* The State of Local News Project, 2023. https://localnewsinitiative.northwestern.edu/projects/state-of-local-news/2023/report/; UNC Hussman School of Journalism and Media. "Do You Live in a News Desert?" https://www.usnewsdeserts.com/#viz1626105082044.

Notes

3. Masta, K. E. "More Americans Are Getting News on TikTok, Bucking the Trend Seen on Most Other Social Media Sites." Pew Research Center, November 15, 2023. https://www.pewresearch.org/short-reads/2023/11/15/more-americans-are-getting-news-on-tiktok-bucking-the-trend-seen-on-most-other-social-media-sites/.

4. "American Views 2020: Trust, Media, and Democracy, A Deepening Divide." Gallup/Knight Foundation, August 2020. https://knightfoundation.org/wp-content/uploads/2020/08/American-Views-2020-Trust-Media-and-Democracy.pdf.

5. Klein, E. *Why We're Polarized*. New York: Simon & Schuster, 2020.

6. Gottfried, J, and Liedke, J. "Partisan Divides in Media Trust Widen, Driven by a Decline among Republicans." Pew Research Center, August 30, 2021. https://www.pewresearch.org/short-reads/2021/08/30/partisan-divides-in-media-trust-widen-driven-by-a-decline-among-republicans/.

7. Centers for Disease Control and Prevention. "COVID Data Tracker." https://covid.cdc.gov/covid-data-tracker/#vaccinations_vacc-people-booster-percent-pop5. Retrieved October 18, 2023.

8. Perkins H. W. "Social Norms and the Prevention of Alcohol Misuse in Collegiate Contexts." *Journal of Studies on Alcohol Supplement* 14 (2002): 164–172. https://doi.org/10.15288/jsas.2002.s14.164.

9. Krupnikov, Y., and Ryan, J. B. *The Other Divide: Polarization and Disengagement in American Politics*. Cambridge: Cambridge University Press, 2022.

10. Rozado, D., and Kaufmann, E. "The Increasing Frequency of Terms Denoting Political Extremism in U.S. and U.K. News Media." *Social Sciences* 11, no. 4 (2022): 167. http://dx.doi.org/10.3390/socsci11040167.

11. Beckett, L. "How Leftwing Media Focus on Far-Right Groups Is Helping to Normalize Hate." *The Guardian*, March 5, 2017. https://www.theguardian.com/world/2017/mar/05/left-wing-media-far-right-normalize-hate-trump.

12. Tager, J., and Lopez, S. *Hate in the Headlines: Journalism and the Challenge of Extremism*. PEN America, 2022. https://pen.org/report/hate-in-the-headlines/#.

13. Robison, J., and Mullinix, K. J. "Elite Polarization and Public Opinion: How Polarization Is Communicated and Its Effects." *Political Communication* 33, no. 2 (2016): 261–282. https://doi.org/10.1080/10584609.2015.1055526.

14. Druckman, J. N., Klar, S., Krupnikov, Y., Levendusky, M., and Ryan, J. B. "(Mis)estimating Affective Polarization." *The Journal of Politics* 84, no. 2 (2022): 1106–1117. https://doi.org/10.1086/715603.

15. Yudkin, D., Hawkins, S., and Dixon, T. "The Perception Gap: How False Impressions Are Pulling Americans Apart." More in Common, 2019. https://perceptiongap.us/.

16. "American Views 2020: Trust, Media, and Democracy, A Deepening Divide." Gallup/Knight Foundation, August 2020. https://knightfoundation.org/wp-content/uploads/2020/08/American-Views-2020-Trust-Media-and-Democracy.pdf

17. Allen, J., Howland, B., Mobius, M., Rothschild, D., and Watts, D. J. "Evaluating the Fake News Problem at the Scale of the Information Ecosystem." *Science Advances* 6, no. 14 (2020). https://doi.org/10.1126/sciadv.aay3539.

18. Lawson, M. A., Anand, S., and Kakkar, H. "Tribalism and Tribulations: The Social Costs of Not Sharing Fake News." *Journal of Experimental Psychology: General* 152, no. 3 (2023): 611–631. https://doi.org/10.1037/xge0001374.

19. "American Views 2020."

20. Bago, B., Rand, D. G., and Pennycook, G. "Fake News, Fast and Slow: Deliberation Reduces Belief in False (But Not True) News Headlines." *Journal of Experimental Psychology: General* 149, no. 8 (2020): 1608–1613. https://doi.org/10.1037/xge0000729.

21. Jolls, T., and Thoman, E. *Literacy for the 21st Century: An Overview & Orientation to Media Literacy Education* (2nd edition). Center for Media Literacy, 2008. https://www.medialit.org/sites/default/files/01a_mlkorientation_rev2_0.pdf.

22. Weir, K. "Why We Fall for Fake News: Hijacked Thinking or Laziness?" American Psychological Association, 2020. https://www.apa.org/news/apa/2020/fake-news.

23. Jurkowitz, M., Mitchell, A., Shearer, E., and Walker, M. "U.S. Media Polarization and the 2020 Election: A Nation Divided." Pew Research Center, January 24, 2020. https://www.pewresearch.org/journalism/2020/01/24/u-s-media-polarization-and-the-2020-election-a-nation-divided/.

24. Forde, S. L., Gutsche, R. E., and Pinto, J. "Exploring 'Ideological Correction' in Digital News Updates of Portland Protests & Police Violence." *Journalism* 24, no. 1 (2023): 157–176. https://doi.org/10.1177/14648849221100073.

25. Broockman, D., and Kalla, J. "Consuming Cross-Cutting Media Causes Learning and Moderates Attitudes: A Field Experiment with Fox News Viewers." *OSF Preprints* (April 1, 2022). https://doi.org/10.31219/osf.io/jrw26.

26. Fitzgerald, K., Green, M., and Paravati, E. "Restorative Narratives: Using Narrative Projectory for Prosocial Outcomes." *The Journal of Public Interest Communications* 4, no. 51 (2020). https://doi.org/10.32473/jpic.v4.i2.p51.

27. Peters, N. (2023). "Restorative Narratives: Defining a New Strength-Based Genre." IVOH, April 13, 2023. https://ivoh.org/restorativenarrative/.

28. McGonigal, K. *The Upside of Stress: Why Stress Is Good for You and How to Get Good at It.* New York: Avery, 2016.

Chapter 3

1. Wong, B. "Top Social Media Trends of 2023." *Forbes Advisor*, 2023. https://www.forbes.com/advisor/business/social-media-statistics/; Olmstead, K., Lampe, C., and Ellison, N. B. "Social Media and the Workplace." Pew Research Center, June 22, 2016. https://www.pewresearch.org/internet/2016/06/22/social-media-and-the-workplace/.

2. Dinesh, S., and Odabaş M. "8 Facts about Americans and Twitter as It Rebrands to X." Pew Research Center, July 26, 2023. https://www.pewresearch.org/short-reads/2023/07/26/8-facts-about-americans-and-twitter-as-it-rebrands-to-x/.

3. Dean, B. "TikTok Statistics You Need to Know in 2024." Backlinko, 2023. https://backlinko.com/tiktok-users.

4. Statista. "Average Time Spent Per Day on Select Social Media Platforms in the United States in 2023." https://www.statista.com/statistics/1301075/us-daily-time-spent-social-media-platforms/.

5. Barrett, P. M., Hendrix, J., and Sims, J. G. "Fueling the Fire: How Social Media Intensifies U.S. Political Polarization and What Can Be Done about It." NYU Stern Center for Business and Human Rights, 2021. https://bhr.stern.nyu.edu/polarization-report-page.

6. Gudka, M., Gardiner, K. L. K., and Lomas, T. "Towards a Framework for Flourishing through Social Media: A Systematic Review of 118 Research Studies." *The Journal of Positive Psychology* 18, no. 1 (2023): 86–105. https://doi.org/10.1080/17439760.2021.1991447.

7. McClain, C., Widjaya, R., Rivero, G., and Smith, A. "The Behaviors and Attitudes of U.S. Adults on Twitter." Pew Research Center, November 15, 2021. https://www.pewresearch.org/internet/2021/11/15/the-behaviors-and-attitudes-of-u-s-adults-on-twitter/.

8. Bestvater, S., and Shah, S. "4 Facts about Political Tweets Shared by U.S. Adults." Pew Research Center, June 30, 2022. https://www.pewresearch.org/short-reads/2022/06/30/5-facts-about-political-tweets-shared-by-u-s-adults/.

9. Hughes, A. "A Small Majority of Prolific Users Account for a Majority of Political Tweets Sent by U.S. Adults." Pew Research Center, October 23, 2019. https://www.pewresearch.org/short-reads/2019/10/23/a-small-group-of-prolific-users-account-for-a-majority-of-political-tweets-sent-by-u-s-adults/.

10. Saveski, M., Gillani, N., Yuan, A., Vijayaraghavan, P., and Roy, D. "Perspective-Taking to Reduce Affective Polarization on Social Media." *Proceedings of the International AAAI Conference on Web and Social Media* 16, no. 1 (2022): 885–895. https://doi.org/10.1609/icwsm.v16i1.19343.

11. Bestvater and Shah. "4 Facts about Political Tweets."

12. Bail, C. A., Argyle, L. P., Brown, T. W., Bumpus, J. P. et al. "Exposure to Opposing Views Can Increase Political Polarization: Evidence from a Large-Scale Field Experiment on Social Media." *PNAS* 37 (2018): 9216–9221. https://doi.org/10.1073/pnas.1804840115.

Notes

13. Kubin, E., and Sikorski, C. "The Role of (Social) Media in Political Polarization: A Systematic Review." *Annals of the International Communication Association* 45, no. 3 (2021): 188–206. https://doi.org/10.1080/23808985.2021.1976070.

14. Bor, A., and Petersen, M. B. "The Psychology of Online Political Hostility: A Comprehensive, Cross-National Test of the Mismatch Hypothesis." *American Political Science Review*, 116, no. 1 (2022): 1-18.

15. Barrett, Hendrix, and Sims. "Fueling the Fire."

16. Van Bavel, J. J., Rathje, S., Harris, E., Robertson, C., and Sternisko, A. "How Social Media Shapes Polarization." *Trends in Cognitive Sciences* 25, no. 11 (2021): 913–916. https://doi.org/10.1016/j.tics.2021.07.013.

17. Allcott, H., Braghieri, L., Eichmeyer, S., and Gentzkow, M. "The Welfare Effects of Social Media." *American Economic Review* 110, no. 3 (2020): 629–676. https://doi.org/10.1257/aer.20190658.

18. Kupferschmidt, K. "Studies Find Little Impact of Social Media on Polarization." *Science* 381, no. 6656 (July 28, 2023): 367–368. DOI: 10.1126/science.adj9569.

19. Levy, R. "Social Media, News Consumption, and Polarization: Evidence from a Field Experiment." *American Economic Review* 111, no. 3 (2021): 831–70. https://doi.org/10.1257/aer.20191777.

20. Odabaş, M. "5 Facts about Twitter 'Lurkers.'" Pew Research Center, March 16, 2022. https://www.pewresearch.org/short-reads/2022/03/16/5-facts-about-twitter-lurkers/.

21. Saveski, M., Gillani, N., Yuan, A., Vijayaraghavan, P., and Roy, D. "Perspective-Taking to Reduce Affective Polarization on Social Media." *Proceedings of the International AAAI Conference on Web and Social Media* 16, no. 1 (2022): 885–895. https://doi.org/10.1609/icwsm.v16i1.19343.

22. Friedman, W., and Schleifer, D. *America's Hidden Common Ground on Overcoming Divisiveness: Charting a Path Forward.* Public Agenda, 2021. https://publicagenda.org/wp-content/uploads/HCG-Overcoming-Divisiveness-2021.pdf.

23. Muhammed T, S., and Mathew, S. K. "The Disaster of Misinformation: A Review of Research in Social Media." *International Journal of Data Science and Analytics* 13, no. 4 (2022): 271–285. https://doi.org/10.1007/s41060-022-00311-6.

24. Muhammed and Mathew. (2022). "The Disaster of Misinformation."

25. Lawson, M. A., Anand, S., and Kakkar, H. (2023). "Tribalism and Tribulations: The Social Costs of Not Sharing Fake News." *Journal of Experimental Psychology: General* 152, no. 3 (2023): 611–631. https://doi.org/10.1037/xge0001374.

26. Center for Countering Digital Hate. "How to Navigate Online Disinformation and Propaganda and Practice Information Resilience." 2023. https://counterhate.com/blog/how-to-navigate-online-disinformation-and-propaganda-and-practicing-information-resilience/.

27. Van Kampen, K. *The SIFT Method*. The University of Chicago Library, 2023. https://guides.lib.uchicago.edu/misinformation.

28. Cho, H., Cannon, J., Lopez, R., and Li, W. "Social Media Literacy: A Conceptual Framework." *New Media & Society* (2022). https://doi.org/10.1177/14614448211068530.

29. Pew Research Center. "Mobile Fact Sheet." January 31, 2024. https://www.pewresearch.org/internet/fact-sheet/mobile/.

30. Duhigg, C. *The Power of Habit: Why We Do What We Do in Life and Business*. New York: Random House, 2014.

31. Hankock, J. T., Liu, S. X., Luo, M., and Mieczkowski, H. "Social Media and Psychological Well-Being." In S. C. Matz (ed.) *The Psychology of Technology*. Washington, DC: American Psychological Association, 2022.

32. American Psychological Association. "Health Advisory on Social Media Use in Adolescence." 2023. https://www.apa.org/topics/social-media-internet/health-advisory-adolescent-social-media-use.

33. Tufekci, Z. "How Social Media Took Us from Tahrir Square to Donald Trump." *MIT Technology Review*, August 14, 2018. https://www.technologyreview.com/2018/08/14/240325/how-social-media-took-us-from-tahrir-square-to-donald-trump/.

34. Groshek, J., and Bronda, S. "How Social Media Can Distort and Misinform When Communicating Science." The Conversation, 2016. https://theconversation.com/how-social-media-can-distort-and-misinform-when-communicating-science-59044.

35. Woolley, K., and Sharif, M. A. "The Psychology of Your Scrolling Addiction." *Harvard Business Review*, January 2022. https://hbr.org/2022/01/the-psychology-of-your-scrolling-addiction.

36. Center for Humane Technology. "Control Your Tech Use." https://www.humanetech.com/take-control.

Chapter 4

1. Gehlbach, H., and Vriesema, C. C. "Meta-Bias: A Practical Theory of Motivated Thinking." *Educational Psychology Review* 31 (2019): 65-85. https://doi.org/10.1007/s10648-018-9454-6.

2. Roets, A., and Van Hiel, A. "Allport's Prejudiced Personality Today: Need for Closure as the Motivated Cognitive Basis of Prejudice." *Current Directions in Psychological Science* 20, no. 6 (2011): 349-354. https://doi.org/10.1177/0963721411424894.

3. Grant, A. *Think Again: The Power of Knowing What You Don't Know*. New York: Viking, 2021.

4. Fast, L. A., Reimer, H. M., and Funder, D. C. "The Social Behavior and Reputation of the Attributionally Complex." *Journal of Research in Personality* 42 (2008): 208-222.

5. Nickerson, R. S. "Confirmation Bias: A Ubiquitous Phenomenon in Many Guises." *Review of General Psychology* 2, no. 2 (1998): 175–220. https://doi.org/10.1037/1089-2680.2.2.175.

6. Ross, L., and Ward, A. "Naive Realism in Everyday Life: Implications for Social Conflict and Misunderstanding." In E. S. Reed, E. Turiel, and T. Brown (eds.). *Values and Knowledge*. Mahwah, NJ: Lawrence Erlbaum Associates, Inc., 1996, pp. 103–135.

7. Waytz, A., Young, L. L., and Ginges, J. "Motive Attribution Asymmetry for Love vs. Hate Drives Intractable Conflict." *Proceedings of the National*

Academy of Sciences 111, no. 4 (2014): 15687-15692. https://doi.org/10.1073/pnas.1414146111.

8. Pasek M .H., Ankori-Karlinsky L. O., Levy-Vene A., and Moore-Berg S. L. "Misperceptions about Out-Partisans' Democratic Values May Erode Democracy." *Scientific Reports* 12 (2022): 16284. https://doi.org/10.1038/s41598-022-19616-4.

9. Moore-Berg, S. L., Ankori-Karlinsky, L., Hameiri, B., and Bruneau, E. "Exaggerated Meta-Perceptions Predict Intergroup Hostility between American Political Partisans." *Proceedings of the National Academy of Sciences* 117, no. 26 (2020): 14864-14872. https://doi.org/10.1073/pnas.2001263117.

10. Strengthening Democracy Challenge. "Winning Interventions: List of Winners." Stanford University. https://www.strengtheningdemocracychallenge.org/winning-interventions.

11. Roets and Van Hiel. "Allport's Prejudiced Personality Today."

Part II

1. Grimaud, J. "Where Is Moana From? The Home and Heritage of Moana." *FamilySearch Blog*, January 8, 2021. https://www.familysearch.org/en/blog/where-is-moana-from.

Chapter 5

1. "Understanding the Stress Response." Harvard Health Publishing, July 6, 2020. https://www.health.harvard.edu/staying-healthy/understanding-the-stress-response.

2. Mariotti A. "The Effects of Chronic Stress on Health: New Insights into the Molecular Mechanisms of Brain–Body Communication." *Future Science OA* 1, no. 3 (2015). https://doi.org/10.4155/fso.15.21; Chrousos G. P. "Stress and Disorders of the Stress System." *Nature Reviews Endocrinology* 5, no. 7 (2009): 374–381. https://doi.org/10.1038/nrendo.2009.106.

Notes

3. Smith, K.B., Hibbing, M.V., and Hibbing, J.R. "Friends, Relatives, Sanity, and Health: The Costs of Politics." *PLoS ONE* 14, no. 9 (2019): e0221870. https://doi.org/10.1371/journal.pone.0221870; Fraser, T., Aldrich, D. P., Panagopoulos, C., Hummel, D., and Kim, D. "The Harmful Effects of Partisan Polarization on Health." *PNAS Nexus* 1, no. 1 (2022): 1–10. https://doi.org/10.1093/pnasnexus/pgac011; Ford, B. Q., Feinberg, M., Lassetter, B., and Gatchpazian, A. "The Political is Personal: The Costs of Daily Politics." *Journal of Personality and Social Psychology* (2023).

4. American Psychological Association. "Stress in America." 2022. https://www.apa.org/news/press/releases/stress/2022/concerned-future-inflation.

5. Smith , K.B. "Politics Is Making Us Sick: The Negative Impact of Political Engagement on Public Health during the Trump Administration." *PLoS ONE* 17, no. 1 (2022): e0262022. https://doi.org/10.1371/journal.pone.0262022.

6. Robertson, D. "How 'Owning the Libs' Became the GOP's Core Belief." *Politico*, March 21, 2021. https://www.politico.com/news/magazine/2021/03/21/owning-the-libs-history-trump-politics-pop-culture-477203.

7. Bonanno, G. A. *The End of Trauma. How the New Science of Resilience Is Changing How We Think about PTSD*. New York: Basic Books, 2021.

8. Stanislawski, K. "The Coping Circumplex Model: An Integrative Model of the Structure of Coping with Stress." *Frontiers in Psychology* 10 (2019). https://doi.org/10.3389/fpsyg.2019.00694.

9. Menschner, C., and Maul, A. "Key Ingredients for Successful Trauma-Informed Care Implementation." Center for Health Care Strategies, 2016. https://www.chcs.org/resource/key-ingredients-for-successful-trauma-informed-care-implementation/.

10. Schmitt, M., Gollwitzer, M., Maes, J., and Arbach, D. "Justice Sensitivity: Assessment and Location in the Personality Space." *European Journal of Psychological Assessment* 21, no. 3 (2005): 202–211. https://doi.org/10.1027/1015-5759.21.3.202; Gabay, R., Hameiri, B., Rubel-Lifschitz, T., and Nadler, A. "The Tendency for Interpersonal Victimhood: The Personality Construct and Its Consequences." *Personality and Individual Differences* 165 (2020). https://doi.org/10.1016/j.paid.2020.110134.

11. Armaly, M.T., Buckley, D.T., and Enders, A.M. "Christian Nationalism and Political Violence: Victimhood, Racial Identity, Conspiracy, and Support for the Capitol Attacks." *Political Behavior* 44 (2022): 937–960. https://doi .org/10.1007/s11109-021-09758-y.

12. Wohl, M. J., and Branscombe, N. R. "Remembering Historical Victimization: Collective Guilt for Current Ingroup Transgressions." *Journal of Personality and Social Psychology* 94, no. 6 (2008): 988–1006. https://doi.org/10.1037/ 0022-3514.94.6.988.

13. Kaufman, S. B. "Unraveling the Mindset of Victimhood." *Scientific American*, 2020. https://www.scientificamerican.com/article/unraveling-the-mindset -of-victimhood/.

14. Katarzyna, J., LaFree, G., Piazza, J., and Becker, M.H. "A Comparison of Political Violence by Left-Wing, Right-Wing, and Islamic Extremists in the United States and the World." *PNAS* 119, no. 30 (2022). https://doi .org/10.1073/pnas.2122593119.

15. American Psychological Association. "Stress in America."

16. NcNamee. S. J. *The Meritocracy Myth* (Fourth Edition). Lanham, MD: Rowman & Littlefield, 2018.

17. Israel, T. "Exploring Privilege in Counseling Psychology: Shifting the Lens." *The Counseling Psychologist* 40 (2012): 158-180. https://doi .org/10.1177/0011000011426297.

18. Lohr, J. M., Olatunji, B. O., Baumeister, R. F., and Bushman, B. J. "The Psychology of Venting Anger and Empirically Supported Alternatives That Do No Harm." *Scientific Review of Mental Health Practice* 5, no. 1 (2007): 53-64.

19. Lohr, Olatunji, Baumeister, and Bushman. "The Psychology of Venting Anger."

20. Stanislawski. "The Coping Circumplex Model."

21. Stanislawski. "The Coping Circumplex Model."

22. Perciavalle, V., Blandini, M., Fecarotta, P., Buscemi, A., Di Corrado, D., Bertolo, L., Fichera, F., and Coco, M. "The Role of Deep Breathing on Stress." *Neurological Sciences* 38, no. 3 (2017): 451–458. https://doi.org/10.1007/ s10072-016-2790-8; Toussaint, L., Nguyen, Q. A., Roettger, C., Dixon, K.,

Notes

Offenbächer, M., Kohls, N., Hirsch, J., and Sirois, F. (2021). "Effectiveness of Progressive Muscle Relaxation, Deep Breathing, and Guided Imagery in Promoting Psychological and Physiological States of Relaxation." *Evidence-Based Complementary and Alternative Medicine: eCAM* (2021): 5924040. https://doi.org/10.1155/2021/5924040.

23. Jackson, Erica M. "Stress Relief: The Role of Exercise in Stress Management." *ACSM's Health & Fitness Journal* 17, no. 3 (2013): 14-19. http://dx.doi.org/10.1249/FIT.0b013e31828cb1c9.

24. Cotman, C. W., Berchtold, N. C., and Christie, L. A. "Exercise Builds Brain Health: Key Roles of Growth Factor Cascades and Inflammation." *Trends in Neurosciences* 30, no. 9 (2007): 464–472. https://doi.org/10.1016/j.tins.2007.06.011.

25. Creswell J. D. "Mindfulness Interventions." *Annual Review of Psychology* 68 (2017): 491–516. https://doi.org/10.1146/annurev-psych-042716-051139.

26. Ford, Feinberg, Lassetter, Thai, and Gatchpazian. "The Political is Personal."

27. Southwick, S. M., Sippel, L., Krystal, J., Charney, D., Mayes, L., and Pietrzak, R. "Why Are Some Individuals More Resilient Than Others: The Role of Social Support." *World Psychiatry* 15, no. 1 (2016): 77–79. https://doi.org/10.1002/wps.20282.

28. Ozbay, F., Johnson, D. C., Dimoulas, E., Morgan, C. A., Charney, D., and Southwick, S. (2007). "Social Support and Resilience to Stress: From Neurobiology to Clinical Practice." *Psychiatry* 4, no. 5 (2007): 35-40.

29. Coan, J. A., Kasle, S. Jackson, A. Schaefer, H. S., and Davidson, R. J. "Mutuality and the Social Regulation of Neural Threat Responding." *Attachment & Human Development* 15, no. 3 (2013): 303-315. https://doi.org/10.1080/14616734.2013.782656.

30. Suttie, J. "Does Venting Your Feelings Actually Help?" *Greater Good Magazine*, 2021. https://greatergood.berkeley.edu/article/item/does_venting_your_feelings_actually_help.

31. McGonigal, K. *The Upside of Stress: Why Stress Is Good for You and How to Get Good at It.* New York: Avery, 2016.

32. Bonanno. *The End of Trauma.*

33. McGonigal. *The Upside of Stress.*

34. Taylor, S. E. "Tend and Befriend Theory." In P. A. M. Van Lange, A. W. Kruglanski, and E. T. Higgins (eds.). *Handbook of Theories of Social Psychology.* London: SAGE Publications Ltd, 2012, pp. 32–49. https://doi.org/10.4135/9781446249215.n3.

35. McGonigal. *The Upside of Stress.*

36. Kobylińska, D., and Petko, K. "Flexible Emotion Regulation: How Situational Demands and Individual Differences Influence the Effectiveness of Regulatory Strategies." *Frontiers in Psychology* 10 (2019). https://doi.org/10.3389/fpsyg.2019.00072.

37. Bonanno. *The End of Trauma.*

38. Butler, E. A., Lee, T. L., and Gross, J. J. "Emotion Regulation and Culture: Are the Social Consequences of Emotion Suppression Culture-Specific?" *Emotion* 7 (2009): 30–48.

39. Stanislawski. "The Coping Circumplex Model."

40. McGonigal. *The Upside of Stress.*

41. McGonigal. *The Upside of Stress.*

Chapter 6

1. Ballantyne, N. "Recent Work on Intellectual Humility: A Philosopher's Perspective." *The Journal of Positive Psychology* 18, no. 2 (2023): 200-220. https://doi.org/ 10.1080/17439760.2021.1940252; Gehlbach, H., Robinson, C. D., & Fletcher, A. (Preprint). "The Illusion of Information Adequacy: A Corollary to Naïve Realism." *PsyArXiv* (2023). https://osf.io/preprints/psyarxiv/fdu3m/.

2. Anson, I.G. "Partisanship, Political Knowledge, and the Dunning-Kruger Effect." *Political Psychology* 39 (2018): 1173-1192. https://doi-org.proxy.library.ucsb.edu/10.1111/pops.12490.

3. Porter, T., and Schumann, K. "Intellectual Humility and Openness to the Opposing View." *Self and Identity* 17, no. 2 (2018): 139-162. https://doi.org/10.1080/15298868.2017.1361861.

4. Ballantyne. "Recent Work on Intellectual Humility."

5. Hagá, S., and Olson, K. R. "'If I Only Had a Little Humility, I Would Be Perfect': Children's and Adults' Perceptions of Intellectually Arrogant, Humble, and Diffident People." *The Journal of Positive Psychology* 12, no. 1 (2017): 87-98. https://doi.org/10.1080/17439760.2016.1167943.

6. Ballantyne,. "Recent Work on Intellectual Humility."

7. Israel, T., Bettergarcia, J. N., Delucio, K., Avellar, T. R., Harkness, A., and Goodman, J. A. "Reactions of Law Enforcement to LGBTQ Diversity Training." *Human Resource Development Quarterly* 28, no. 2 (2017): 197-226. https://doi.org/10.1002/hrdq.21281.

8. Schwarz, N. "Humility in Inquiry." *The Journal of Positive Psychology* 18, no. 2 (2023): 267-270. https://doi.org/10.1080/17439760.2022.2155225.

9. Porter, T. "The Benefits of Admitting When You Don't Know." *Behavioral Scientist*, April 30, 2018. https://behavioralscientist.org/the-benefits-of-admitting-when-you-dont-know/.

10. Bowes, S. M., and Tasimi, A. "Is Intellectual Humility 'Good' for People?" *The Journal of Positive Psychology* 18, no. 2 (2023): 250-253. http://dx.doi.org/10.1080/17439760.2022.2155226.

11. Gehlbach, H. "A New Perspective on Perspective Taking: A Multidimensional Approach to Conceptualizing an Aptitude." *Educational Psychology Review* 16, no. 3 (September 2004): 207-234. http://dx.doi.org/10.1023/B:EDPR.0000034021.12899.11.

12. Goldstein, N. J., Vezich, I. S., and Shapiro, J. R. (2014). "Perceived Perspective Taking: When Others Walk in Our Shoes." *Journal of Personality and Social Psychology* 106, no. 6 (2014): 941. https://doi.org/10.1037/a0036395.

13. Gehlbach, H., and Mu, N. "How We Understand Others: A Theory of How Social Perspective Taking Unfolds." *Review of General Psychology* 27, no. 3 (2023): 282-302. https://doi.org/10.1177/10892680231152595.

14. Gehlbach and Mu "How We Understand Others: A Theory of How Social Perspective Taking Unfolds."

15. Ames, D. R. "Inside the Mind Reader's Tool Kit: Projection and Stereotyping in Mental State Inference." *Journal of Personality and Social Psychology* 87, no. 3 (2004): 340–353. https://doi.org/10.1037/0022-3514.87.3.340; Gerace A., Day A., Casey S., Mohr P. "Perspective Taking and Empathy: Does Having Similar Past Experience to Another Person Make It Easier to Take Their Perspective?" *Journal of Relationships Research* 6 (2015): e10. https://doi.org/10.1017/jrr.2015.6.

16. Gehlbach, H. "Learning to Walk in Another's Shoes." *Phi Delta Kappan* 98, no 6 (2017): 8–12. https://doi.org/10.1177/0031721717696471.

17. Gehlbach, H., and Brinkworth, M. E. "The Social Perspective Taking Process: Strategies and Sources of Evidence in Taking Another's Perspective." *Teachers College Record* 114, no. 1 (2012): 29.

18. Gehlbach, H., Brinkworth, M. E., and Wang, M.-T. "The Social Perspective Taking Process: What Motivates Individuals to Take Another's Perspective?" *Teachers College Record* 114, no. 1 (2012): 29.

19. Grant, A. *Think Again: The Power of Knowing What You Don't Know.* New York: Viking, 2021.

20. Gehlbach, Brinkworth, and Wang. "The Social Perspective Taking Process."

21. Gehlbach. "Learning to Walk in Another's Shoes."

22. McGregor, S., and Goldman, R. D. "Determinants of Parental Vaccine Hesitancy." *Canadian Family Physician/Le Médecin de famille canadien* 67, no. 5 (2021): 339–341. https://doi.org/10.46747/cfp.6705339.

23. Keinan, R., and Bereby-Meyer, Y. "Perceptions of Active versus Passive Risks, and the Effect of Personal Responsibility." *Personality & Social Psychology Bulletin* 43, no. 7 (2017): 999–1007. https://doi.org/10.1177/0146167217703079.

24. McGregor and Goldman. "Determinants of Parental Vaccine Hesitancy."

25. Nowak, G. J., and Cacciatore, M. A. "State of Vaccine Hesitancy in the United States." *Pediatric Clinics of North America* 70, no. 2 (2023): 197–210. https://doi.org/10.1016/j.pcl.2022.11.001.

26. Israel, T. "Reflecting on why people." Facebook, August 6, 2021. https://www.facebook.com/TaniaIsrael/posts/

Notes

pfbid0jkGM4sYK5psDKbSQmGWFSAApy6fZVHNB6v
Wr1Wq9s1ymZkKjbhkADRxJKdKs8iHh.

27. Ford, B. Q., Feinberg, M., Lassetter, B., Thai, S., and Gatchpazian, A. "The Political is Personal: The Costs of Daily Politics." *Journal of Personality and Social Psychology* 125, no. 1 (2023): 1–28. https://doi.org/10.1037/pspa0000335.

28. Corning, A. F., and Myers, D. J. "Individual Orientation toward Engagement in Social Action." *Political Psychology* 23 (2002): 703-729. https://doi.org/10.1111/0162-895X.00304.

29. Hook, J. N., Hodge, A. S., Watkins, C. E., and DeBlaere, C. "What Motivates Us to Be Intellectually Humble?: A Necessary Bridge to Applied Work." *The Journal of Positive Psychology* 18, no. 2 (2023): 276-279. https://doi.org/10.10 80/17439760.2022.2155223; Gehlbach, H., and Vriesema, C. C. "Meta-Bias: A Practical Theory of Motivated Thinking." *Educational Psychology Review* 31 (2019): 65-85. https://doi.org/10.1007/s10648-018-9454-6.

Chapter 7

1. Simas, E. N., Clifford, S., and Kirkland, J. H. "How Empathic Concern Fuels Political Polarization." *American Political Science Review* 114, no. 1 (2020): 258-269. https://doi.org/10.1017/S0003055419000534.

2. Broockman, D., and Kalla, J. "Durably Reducing Transphobia: A Field Experiment on Door-to-Door Canvassing." *Science*, 352, no. 6282 (2016): 220-224. https://doi.org/10.1126/science.aad9713.

3. McAuliffe, W., Carter, E., Berhane, J., Snihur, A., and McCullough, M. "Is Empathy the Default Response to Suffering? A Meta-Analytic Evaluation of Perspective Taking's Effect on Empathic Concern." *Personality and Social Psychology Review* 24, no. 2 (2020): 141-162. https://doi.org/10.1177/1088868319887599.

4. Batson, C. D., Early, S., and Salvarani, G. "Perspective Taking: Imagining How Another Feels versus Imaging How You Would Feel." *Personality and Social Psychology Bulletin* 23, no. 7 (1997): 751-758. https://doi.org/10.1177/0146167297237008.

5. Seppala, E. "Compassionate Mind, Healthy Body." *Greater Good Magazine*, 2013. https://greatergood.berkeley.edu/article/item/compassionate_mind_healthy_body.

6. Konrath, S., Fuhrel-Forbis, A., Lou, A., and Brown, S. "Motives for Volunteering Are Associated with Mortality Risk in Older Adults." *Health Psychology* 31, no. 1 (2012): 87–96. https://doi.org/10.1037/a0025226.

7. Hawkins, M., and Nadel, J. (eds.). *How Compassion Can Transform Our Politics, Economy, and Society* (First Edition). New York: Routledge, 2021.

8. Brooks, A. C. *Love Your Enemies: How Decent People Can Save America From the Culture of Contempt.* New York: Broadside Books, 2019.

9. Desbordes, G., Gard, T., Hoge, E. A., Hölzel, B. K., Kerr, C., Lazar, S. W., Olendzki, A., and Vago, D. R. "Moving beyond Mindfulness: Defining Equanimity as an Outcome Measure in Meditation and Contemplative Research." *Mindfulness* (January 2014): 356–372. https://doi.org/10.1007/s12671-013-0269-8.

10. Chödrön, Y. K. "Courage." *Prajna Sparks* (podcast), episode 17, 2021. https://www.prajnafire.com/sparks/episode/1ae3ccf8/17-or-courage.

11. Hutcherson, C. A., Seppala, E. M., and Gross, J. J. "Loving-Kindness Meditation Increases Social Connectedness." *Emotion* 8, no. 5 (2008): 720-724. https://doi.org/10.1037/a0013237.

12. Fredrickson, B. L., Boulton, A. J., Firestine, A. M., Van Cappellen, P., Algoe, S. B., Brantley, M. M., . . . Salzberg, S. "Positive Emotion Correlates of Meditation Practice: A Comparison of Mindfulness Meditation and Loving-Kindness Meditation." *Mindfulness* 8, no. 6 (2017): 1623-1633. https://doi.org/10.1007/s12671-017-0735-9.

13. Simonsson, O., Bergljottsdotter, C., Narayanan, J., Fisher, S., Bristow, J., Ormston, R., and Chambers, R. "Mindfulness in Politics: A Qualitative Study on Mindfulness Training in the UK Parliament." *Mindfulness* (2023): 1–9. https://doi.org/10.1007/s12671-023-02156-x.

14. Miron, A. M., Branscombe, N. R., Lishner, D. A., Otradovec, A. C., Frankowski, S., Bowers, H. R., Wierzba, B. L., and Malcore, M. "Group-Level Perspective-Taking Effects on Injustice Standards and Empathic Concern

When the Victims Are Categorized as Outgroup Versus Ingroup." *Basic and Applied Social Psychology* 42, no. 5 (2020): 305-323. https://doi.org/10.1080/01 973533.2020.1768096.

15. Zeng, X., Zheng, Y., Gu, X., Wang, R., and Oei, T. P. "Meditation Quality Matters: Effects of Loving-Kindness and Compassion Meditations on Subjective Well-Being Are Associated with Meditation Quality." *Journal of Happiness Studies* 24, no. 1 (2023): 211-229. https://doi.org/10.1007/ s10902-022-00582-7.

Part III

1. U.S. Surgeon General. *Our Epidemic of Loneliness and Isolation: The U.S. Surgeon General's Advisory on the Healing Effects of Social Connection and Community.* Office of the U.S. Surgeon General, 2023. https://www.hhs.gov/sites/default/ files/surgeon-general-social-connection-advisory.pdf

2. Friedman, W., and Schleifer, D. *America's Hidden Common Ground on Overcoming Divisiveness: Charting a Path Forward.* Public Agenda, 2021. https://publicagenda.org/wp-content/uploads/HCG-Overcoming -Divisiveness-2021.pdf.

Chapter 8

1. Tania Israel's Post. LinkedIn. https://www.linkedin.com/posts/tania -israel_conversationsthatmatter-communication-betterconversations -activity-6912490651913785344-Jcgu/; Israel, T. "In the past year, have you had a conversation." Twitter/X, March 23, 2022. https://twitter.com/ TaniaIsraelPhD/status/1506728314550980609.

2. Van Tongeren, D. R., Green, J. D., Hulsey, T. L., Legare, C. H., Bromley, D. G., and Houtman, A. M. "A Meaning-Based Approach to Humility: Relationship Affirmation Reduces Worldview Defense" *Journal of Psychology and Theology,* 42, no. 1 (2014): 62–69. https://doi.org/10.1177/ 009164711404200107.

3. Yeomans, M., Minson, J., Collins, H., Chen, F., and Gino, F. "Conversational Receptiveness: Improving Engagement with Opposing Views." *Organizational Behavior and Human Decision Processes* 160 (2020): 131-148. https://doi .org/10.1016/j.obhdp.2020.03.011.

4. Bruneau, E. G., and Saxe, R. "The Power of Being Heard: The Benefits of 'Perspective-Giving' in the Context of Intergroup Conflict." *Journal of Experimental Social Psychology* 48, no. 4 (2012): 855-866. https://doi .org/10.1016/j.jesp.2012.02.017.

5. Livingstone, A. G., Fernández Rodríguez, L., and Rothers, A. "'They Just Don't Understand Us': The Role of Felt Understanding in Intergroup Relations." *Journal of Personality and Social Psychology* 119, no. 3 (2020): 633-656. https://doi.org/10.1037/pspi0000221.

6. Chen, F. S., Minson, J. A., and Tormala, Z. L. "Tell Me More: The Effects of Expressed Interest on Receptiveness During Dialog." *Journal of Experimental Social Psychology* 46, no. 5 (2010): 850–853. https://doi.org/10.1016/ j.jesp.2010.04.012.

7. Murphy, K. *You're Not Listening: What You're Missing and Why It Matters.* New York: Celadon Books, 2019, p. 86.

8. Itzchakov, G., Kluger, A. N., and Castro, D. R. "I Am Aware of My Inconsistencies but Can Tolerate Them: The Effect of High Quality Listening on Speakers' Attitude Ambivalence." *Personality and Social Psychology Bulletin* 43, no. 1 (2017): 105-120. https://doi .org/10.1177/0146167216675339.

9. Tania Israel's Post. LinkedIn. https://www.linkedin.com/posts/ tania-israel_commonground-perspectivematters-listenfirst-activity -6899784307120975872-KxY0/.

10. Feinberg, M., and Willer, R. "From Gulf to Bridge: When Do Moral Arguments Facilitate Political Influence?" *Personality & Social Psychology Bulletin* 41, no. 12 (2015): 1665–1681. https://doi.org/10.1177/0146167215607842.

11. Schreiner, C., Appel, M., Isberner, M. B., and Richter, T. "Argument Strength and the Persuasiveness of Stories." *Discourse Processes* 55, no. 4 (2017): 371–386. https://doi-org.proxy.library.ucsb.edu/10.1080/016385 3X.2016.1257406.

Notes

12. Kubin, E., Puryear, C., Schein, C., and Gray, K. "Personal Experiences Bridge Moral and Political Divides Better Than Facts." *Proceedings of the National Academy of Sciences of the United States of America* 118, no. 6 (2021): e2008389118. https://doi.org/10.1073/pnas.2008389118.

13. Green, M. C., and Brock, T. C. "The Role of Transportation in the Persuasiveness of Public Narratives." *Journal of Personality and Social Psychology*, 79, no. 5 (2000): 701–721. https://doi.org/10.1037/0022-3514.79.5.701; LaBar, K. S., and Cabeza, R. "Cognitive Neuroscience of Emotional Memory." *Nature Reviews* 7, no. 1 (2006): 54–64. https://doi.org/10.1038/nrn1825.

14. Israel, T. "Exploring Privilege in Counseling Psychology: Shifting the Lens." *The Counseling Psychologist* 40 (2012): 158-180. https://doi.org/10.1177/0011000011426297.

15. Bruneau, E. G., and Saxe, R. "The Power of Being Heard: The Benefits of 'Perspective-Giving' in the Context of Intergroup Conflict." *Journal of Experimental Social Psychology* 48, no. 4 (2012): 855-866. https://doi.org/10.1016/j.jesp.2012.02.017.

16. Santoro, E., and Broockman, D. E. "The Promise and Pitfalls of Cross-Partisan Conversations for Reducing Affective Polarization: Evidence from Randomized Experiments." *Science Advances* 8, no. 25 (2022): eabn5515. https://doi.org/10.1126/sciadv.abn5515.

Chapter 9

1. McCoy, J. *What Happens When Democracies Become Perniciously Polarized?* Carnegie Endowment for International Peace, 2022. https://carnegieendowment.org/2022/01/18/what-happens-when-democracies-become-perniciously-polarized-pub-86190; Repucci, S. *From Crisis to Reform: A Call to Strengthen America's Battered Democracy.* Freedom House, 2021. https://freedomhouse.org/report/special-report/2021/crisis-reform-call-strengthen-americas-battered-democracy.

2. Pasek, M.H., Ankori-Karlinsky, LO., Levy-Vene, A. et al. "Misperceptions about Out-Partisans' Democratic Values May Erode Democracy." *Scientific Reports* 12 (2022): 16284. https://doi.org/10.1038/s41598-022-19616-4.

3. Foa, R. S., and Mounk, Y. "The Danger of Deconsolidation." *Journal of Democracy* 27, no. 3 (2016): 5-17. https://www.journalofdemocracy.org/articles/the-danger-of-deconsolidation-the-democratic-disconnect/.

4. Atwell, M. N., Stillerman, B., and Bridgeland, J. M. "Civic Health Index 2021: Citizenship during Crisis." Civic, 2021. https://www.civicllc.com/_files/ugd/03cac8_9d6c072c6df948ff9e003424f51437b2.pdf.

5. Obama. B. "President Obama's Farewell Address." 2017. https://obamawhitehouse.archives.gov/farewell.

6. Desjardins, J. "Mapped: The World's Oldest Democracies." World Economic Forum, August 2019. https://www.weforum.org/agenda/2019/08/countries-are-the-worlds-oldest-democracies/.

7. Gilman, H. R., and Souris, E. "Global Answers for Local Problems: Lessons from Civically Engaged Cities." New America, 2010. https://www.newamerica.org/political-reform/reports/global-answers-local-problems-lessons-civically-engaged-cities/.

8. Desilver, D. "Turnout Soared in 2020 as Nearly Two-Thirds of Eligible U.S. Voters Cast Ballots for President." Pew Research Center, January 28, 2021. https://www.pewresearch.org/short-reads/2021/01/28/turnout-soared-in-2020-as-nearly-two-thirds-of-eligible-u-s-voters-cast-ballots-for-president/.

9. Pew Research Center. "Who Votes, Who Doesn't, and Why: Regular Voters Intermittent Voters, and Those Who Don't." October 18, 2006. https://www.pewresearch.org/politics/2006/10/18/who-votes-who-doesnt-and-why/.

10. Smith, M. A. "Voter Fraud or Voter Suppression? Using Political Science to Evaluate Competing Claims." Midwest Political Science Association, 2020. https://www.mpsanet.org/voter-fraud-or-voter-suppression-using-political-science-to-evaluate-competing-claims/.

11. Hartig, H., Daniller, A., Keeter, S., and Van Green, T. "Republican Gains in 2022 Midterms Driven Mostly by Turnout: An Examination of the 2022 Elections, Based on Validated Voters." Pew Research Center, July 12, 2023. https://www.pewresearch.org/politics/2023/07/12/voting-patterns-in-the-2022-elections/; Center for American Women and Politics. "Gender

Differences in Voter Turnout." https://cawp.rutgers.edu/facts/voters/gender-differences-voter-turnout.

12. Brenan, M. "More Voters Than in Prior Years Say Election Outcome Matters." Gallup, 2020. https://news.gallup.com/poll/322010/voters-prior-years-say-election-outcome-matters.aspx.

13. Woodard, C. "Half of Americans Don't Vote: What Are They Thinking? Inside the Largest Ever Survey of the Politically Disengaged." *Politico*, February 19, 2020. https://www.politico.com/news/magazine/2020/02/19/knight-nonvoter-study-decoding-2020-election-wild-card-115796.

14. Woodard. "Half of Americans Don't Vote."

15. Pew Research Center. "Who Votes, Who Doesn't, and Why."

16. Melotte, S. "Lack of Access to Infrastructure Hurts Voters in Rural America." Governing, April 14, 2023. https://www.governing.com/community/lack-of-access-to-infrastructure-hurts-voter-participation-in-rural-america.

17. Nickerson, D. W., and Rogers, T. "Do You Have a Voting Plan?: Implementation Intentions, Voter Turnout, and Organic Plan Making." *Psychological Science* 21, no. 2 (2010): 194-199. https://doi.org/10.1177/0956797609359326.

18. Woodard. "Half of Americans Don't Vote."

19. Broockman, D.; and Kalla, J. "Durably Reducing Transphobia: A Field Experiment on Door-to-Door Canvassing." *Science*, 352, no. 6282 (2016): 220-224. https://doi.org/10.1126/science.aad9713.

20. Jones, J. M. "Americans Trust Local Government Most, Congress Least." Gallup, 2023. https://news.gallup.com/poll/512651/americans-trust-local-government-congress-least.aspx.

21. U.S. Surgeon General. *Our Epidemic of Loneliness and Isolation: The U.S. Surgeon General's Advisory on the Healing Effects of Social Connection and Community.* Office of the U.S. Surgeon General, 2023. https://www.hhs.gov/sites/default/files/surgeon-general-social-connection-advisory.pdf.

22. Han, H. *How Organizations Develop Activists*. Oxford: Oxford University Press, 2014.

23. Atwell, Stillerman, and Bridgeland. "Civic Health Index 2021."

24. Atwell, Stillerman, and Bridgeland. "Civic Health Index 2021."

25. Rosman, E. "Can Military Service Bridge Social Schisms: The Case of Israel." *Israel Affairs* 26, no. 3 (2020): 348–370. https://doi.org/10.1080/13537121.2020.1754578.

26. Eisner, D., and Gomperts, J. "No Greater Mission. No Greater Means. How National Service Can Advance Bridgebuilding." Convergence. https://convergencepolicy.org/our-work/national-service-bridgebuilding/; New York Times Editorial Board. "Should Young Americans Be Required to Give a Year of Service?" *New York Times*, May 1, 2021. https://www.nytimes.com/2021/05/01/opinion/us-national-service-draft.html.

27. Hammond, J. C. "Slavery, Sectionalism, and the Constitution of 1787." *Commonplace: The Journal of Early American Life*. (2016). https://commonplace.online/article/slavery-sectionalism-1787/.

Chapter 10

1. Listen First Project. "#ListenFirst Coalition." https://www.listenfirstproject.org/listen-first-coalition.

2. Braver Angels. "Our Mission." https://braverangels.org/our-mission/.

3. Baron, H., Blair, R., Choi, D. D., Gamboa, L. et al. "Can Americans Depolarize? Assessing the Effects of Reciprocal Group Reflection on Partisan Polarization" (Unpublished manuscript). 2021. https://doi.org/10.31219/osf.io/3x7z8.

4. Library of Congress. "Gettysburg Address Delivered at Gettysburg Pa. Nov. 19th, 1863. [n. p. n. d.]." https://www.loc.gov/resource/rbpe.24404500/?st=text.

5. Voelkel, J. G., Stagnaro, M., Chu, J., Pink, S. L. et al. "Megastudy Identifying Effective Interventions to Strengthen Americans' Democratic Attitudes." *OSF Preprints* (March 20, 2023). https://doi.org/10.31219/osf.io/y79u5.

6. Information and previews of winning interventions are available at
https://www.strengtheningdemocracychallenge.org/winning-interventions.

7. Problem Solvers Caucus. "About the Caucus." https://problemsolverscaucus
.house.gov/about.

8. Center for Efficient Collaboration. "Transforming Polarized Politics
in the Minnesota State Legislature: A Convergent Facilitation Case
Study." 2015. https://efficientcollaboration.org/wp-content/uploads/
MinnesotaCaseStudy.pdf.

9. George W. Bush Presidential Center. "A Statement from 13 Presidential
Centers." September 7, 2023. https://www.bushcenter.org/publications/
reaffirming-americans-commitment-to-a-more-perfect-union.

10. Bonior, A. "The Health Benefits of Hope: Seeing the Light at the End of
the Tunnel Can Be Very Good for You." *Psychology Today*, March 30, 2021.
https://www.psychologytoday.com/us/blog/friendship-20/202103/
the-health-benefits-hope.

Conclusion

1. *Buffy the Vampire Slayer*. "Chosen," dir. Joss Whedon. May 2, 2003.

About the Author

Tania Israel is a Professor of Counseling Psychology at the University of California, Santa Barbara, and award-winning author of *Beyond Your Bubble: How to Connect Across the Political Divide, Skills and Strategies for Conversations That Work* (APA, 2020). She has shared her work on navigating political polarization with campuses, conferences, corporations, elected officials, and faith communities. Tania has received honors from Congress, the California State Legislature, and the American Psychological Association. Her TEDx talks, podcasts, and *The Flowchart That Will Resolve All Political Conflict in Our Country* can be found on her website, taniaisrael.com. She grew up in Charlottesville, Virginia, and lives in Santa Barbara, California.